Galwey

The Autobiography

The story of a great Irish sportsman

Mick Galwey with Charlie Mulqueen

Published by Irish Rugby Review

Published by: Irish Rugby Review

First published in 2002

Picture Credits:
The Irish Examiner,
Mike McSweeney, Provision Ltd.,
Sportsfile Ltd.,
The Limerick Leader,
Kerrys Eye,
Press 22 Ltd.,
Inpho Ltd.,
Dan Linehan.

Every effort has been made to trace copyright holders and we apologise in advance for any unintentional omissions. We would be pleased to insert the appropriate acknowledgement in future reprints.

Design: Grasshopper Graphics.

Printing: W & G Baird Ltd

ISBN 0-9544106-0-2

FOREWORD

It's not every day that rugby fans get the opportunity to have an insight into the life of one of Ireland's great sporting heroes. This rarity conjures up many emotions for the readers - from envy to nostalgia to infectious sporting passion.

permanent tsb, as proud sponsors of the Irish Rugby team are delighted to sponsor Mick's autobiography, which has all of the above attributes and more.

We congratulate and salute Mick on his book and we take this opportunity to thank him for his immense contribution to all the great sporting moments we have enjoyed over the years, many of which are recounted in this book. I'm sure you will find it a fitting tribute to an honourable and extremely talented sportman.

Brian McConnell
Chief Executive
permanent tsb

CONTENTS

Myself & Joan with Ailbhe and Neasa

INTRODUCTION

IT'S TWILIGHT time for my sporting career and after all that has happened over the past twenty years or so, what is obviously a source of keen disappointment for me is that it is now coming to an end. However, Anno Domini catches up with us all and as I pass my 36th birthday I look back and humbly thank the Lord for giving me a great sporting life. To win an All-Ireland football medal in the green and gold jersey is the dream of every young Kerry lad. Second only to that is a county championship medal. Both are safely tucked away.

To later go on and play rugby 41 times for my country and be chosen to captain the side is almost unbelievable. Then there was the Lions tour to New Zealand in 1993, the 1991 World Cup with Ireland, tours to France, Namibia, New Zealand, Australia, South Africa, Argentina, USA and Canada.

And yet that's not all, far from it. When I first played for Shannon in 1985 and for Munster in 1987, I never imagined what lay in store. I have captained Munster 85 times and represented the province on more than 130 occasions. We reached two Heineken Cup finals and the semi-final of another and while we were unable to satisfy the ambitions of our incredible supporters, I believe we left an indelible mark on the European game.

My years with Shannon have been blessed with many trophies - nine Munster Senior Cups, five AIB League successes and more than a hundred appearances, even two Munster Senior Leagues when that competition meant something. And even though it may be twilight time as we begin season 2002/'03, don't write off the possibility of some more silverware adorning the Galwey household before the boots are hung up for good!

No matter how satisfying it is to win trophies and medals, the friendships you make along the way are just as significant. I like to think that I get on with people. I love a chat, whether with an old pal over a pint in a favourite pub, or with a stranger I might bump into on the street. If they want to talk about Munster rugby or Kerry's prospects in the All-Ireland, that's fine by me.

The nice thing about Irish people is that they know where to draw the line. They won't be slow to express an opinion - like why we didn't change our line-out tactics in rugby or spread the ball more to the wings on the football pitch - but few if any go over the top. And boy, are we good at taking our beating. I will never forget the manner in which the 30,000 fans stood as one at Twickenham after we had lost to Northampton in the final of the 2000 Heineken Cup and cheered and sang and let us know just how much they appreciated our efforts. It was no different two years later at the Millennium Stadium when again we failed to go the final step. By then, we had close on 40,000 people following us. Incredible and humbling.

Many a tear was shed in two wonderful temples of rugby after those disappointments, both on the pitch and in the dressingroom by the players, and in the stands and terraces by the supporters. But never a harsh word, never an accusation that we had let them down, just an acceptance that we had given it our all and that it just wasn't enough.

The same with Ireland. I was fortunate enough to figure on three teams that beat some of the finest sides ever fielded by England. I scored a try at Lansdowne Road in 1993. That kind of thing raises expectation but the honest truth is that a country as small as Ireland and with limited playing resources is unlikely to beat England on a regular basis. While they will hope and dream, the vast majority of Irish people realise this is the case. So when we suffer against the "auld enemy", they appraise the kind of performance we have produced and if they see that everything possible was done, then they leave it at that.

The day that changes will be a sorry one for not just Munster and Ireland but sport in general in this country. In writing this book, I have had the privilege of looking back over countless great occasions both nationally and internationally and they have made me appreciate just how fortunate I've been.

Mick Galwey, November 2002

Try against England. I knew there was somebody on my back, it was Tony Underwood – I was falling from about five yards out – but I got the try.

Heineken Cup Final 2002. Even Ailbhe knows it's not a great day.

BACKSTABBED!

LOSING THE 2000 Heineken Cup final against Northampton Saints at Twickenham in 2000 was bad enough. To fall at the final hurdle again two years later against Leicester Tigers at the magnificent Millennium Stadium was even worse. A new era was dawning, our dynamic coaching team of Declan Kidney and Niall O'Donovan was moving on to even bigger things, my great pal Peter Clohessy was retiring and I was also standing down as captain.

As we shall see, it wasn't easy getting out of Cardiff that night. But that's all we wanted. We were desperately disappointed, so, too, were our legion of supporters. It was good to get back to Limerick but I was so down I hardly had a drink and went to bed early. The feeling of sadness and despondency was even worse the following morning when we had a meeting and said our farewells.

Many of us were going our different directions, especially Declan and Niallo. We made them a presentation and it was a very personal moment for everybody. Some of the lads, of course, had been out all night and never seen the bed but in fairness, they all turned up. Jerry Holland was about the only one of us who could put two words together without breaking down and he was very good. I tried to say that Dec and Niallo had brought us places we had never dreamed of but I'm not too sure I made a very good fist of it! The two lads weren't much better, they could hardly respond because they were so upset and emotional.

That, of course, was perfectly understandable but I often wondered since what the people who followed us throughout Europe and marvelled at the way we could somehow stood up to the biggest, hardest men you ever saw would think if they saw we could be such softies in different circumstances! It didn't have a whole lot to do with losing the final. In fact, we might have been blubbering all the more had we won. It was just that we had an unbelievable camaraderie in the Munster squad and now we were facing into a different and uncertain future.

On the other hand, don't get me wrong. Losing that match at the Millennium Stadium and the way it happened will hurt for many a day to come.

We will always wonder about what might have been had Neil Back played it fair and not cheated at that all-important scrum a few minutes before the finish. He got away with his Hand of God trick, just as Maradona did years before, and the end seemed to justify the means as far as he and his Leicester teammates were concerned. On the other hand, a number of the Tiger fans wrote to the newspapers disowning Back's actions and some even went so far as to state they wouldn't be going to Welford Road again. Back himself must have been a little unhappy because he obviously spent the summer brooding over it and towards the end of August went public for the first time.

"In a way I wish I hadn't done it", he confessed as he looked back on the illegal act of slapping the ball out of Peter Stringer's hands as he attempted to put the ball into a scrum in front of the Tigers posts as they led 15-9 and with time almost up. Back went on: "I have to be honest about it. I don't like people thinking I'm a cheat. I had a lot of mail over the incident, mostly negative. There were letters saying I was a cheat, some of them from Leicester fans, which was a bit hurtful. If people wanted to make me feel bad about what happened, they have. That's disappointing and I know it has upset my wife Alison.

"If I thought there was any possible way of redressing it, I would consider it. I regret it because I don't like to think like that. Because of that one incident, there are people who think I'm a cheat. It has tarnished my reputation. In making any judgment, I would hope people will evaluate me over my whole career and not label me on that one moment. It happened spontaneously. I weighed the options up in a split second and did what I did. I'm very competitive and will do almost anything to win".

So there you are. He says "in a way", he wishes he hadn't done it. That one incident? What about the time he manhandled referee Steve Lander after his last minute penalty try award stole the English Cup from Leicester against Bath back in 1996. If he could redress it, he would "CONSIDER it". It's a strange way to salve your conscience. Neil is right in one respect, though. Quite obviously he WILL do anything to win.

It was cheating. Back said at the time that he did what he had to do. That disappointed me quite a bit. What happens if next time a player does him physical bodily harm and turns around and claims "I did what I had to do so that we would win the match". Go down that road and you're opening a new can of worms.

I've often been asked about the reversal of the roles, if we had been ahead in the same situation and cheated to get out with the win like they did ... would that win be tarnished? I don't want to be a hypocrite here but when a player does something like that, it's something he has to live with. I feel he could have handled it better. Hindsight is a great thing but he got hate mail from Leicester supporters and I myself received a letter from a Leicester supporter stating he was handing his jersey back to Peter Wheeler. This man felt it was cheating and it wasn't on at all.

I suppose it would be worse if we had been ahead and he got away with it and they scored a match winning try. That would be the ultimate, total killer.

Although I couldn't see what actually happened because I had my head buried in the second-row of the scrum, I'll never forget that split second for the rest of my life. A converted try was essential because we were 15-9 behind and I felt we might well get it for we were more than holding our own when we forced that scrum within touching distance of their posts. It was just to the left of the posts, actually, so we called a move that had worked perfectly for us against Cardiff in the Celtic League. All the back line moved to the left and looking at it later, you could see they had one or two on the right. Anthony Foley was to link with Peter Stringer who'd pop it inside for David Wallace who was meant to score under the posts, that's the kind of move it was. No better man than Wally in that situation.

I spoke to him later and as we got down in the scrum, he looked up and saw the gap and felt the move would have worked. But that's something we will never know now. Neil Back stuck his hand in and I didn't realise for a few moments what had happened. Stringer was roaring at the ref and the touch judge but they hadn't seen it. Maybe you couldn't blame them. I remember it happening years ago in a junior match in Castleisland when we were messing around but this was the Heineken European Cup final and it wasn't exactly something you'd be expecting.

The incident didn't cost us the game. We lost because we conceded two tries and they were the better team on the day. At the same time, I'm still sore about it because we could still have won were it not for Back's cheating. That scrum was beside the posts and a try could easily have been converted. On top of that, had the ref spotted what happened, he would certainly have shown Back the yellow card and we would have packed down for another scrum against only seven forwards. The seven pointer was on and that's what hurts most.

It seems that every time we play a big match, there's controversy. We all remember Johnno's (John O'Neill) disallowed try in Lille and he again went over in the corner against Leicester. This time, they had the video ref and he ruled against us. I looked at it afterwards and while he did hit the corner flag, some video refs might have given it. Stranger ones have been awarded - like Brian O'Driscoll's against France and of course we weren't complaining on that occasion!

We started very shakily and Leicester nearly scored in the first few minutes when we were lucky that the French referee Joel Jutge spotted a foul on Dominic Crotty as he ran back to deal with an up and under. They had the edge on us early on but we came back well and Ronan O'Gara kicked a few great penalties. Although our line-out was a bit iffy, we were competing well in the loose and matching them in the scrum which was a big factor. Darren Garforth gave away a few penalties and we stopped their rolling mauls. That was something we had worked really hard on because they had beaten good teams through their mauling alone.

We went in at half time feeling we had a chance but knowing we had

to do better. We were on top for a spell on the restart but then they got a penalty and kicked it to the corner and we thought, here goes, this is their chance. But we stopped them from mauling their way over, I know we gave away a few penalties in the process but we did what we set out to do. To give them their due, they then spread the ball out wide and scored a try and that was a bit of a killer blow. We came back with a penalty and they weren't hammering us but they got the two tries and they were decisive.
Tim Stimpson broke our line early on and Geordan Murphy, my Irish teammate, scored the first and then Austin Healy broke through to touch down between the posts.

We just felt numb at the final whistle. It was harder to take this time. This was another opportunity gone and for some of us it was going to be the last opportunity. Having to walk up the steps once again to collect our losers medals was hard to take. They don't mean much and to be honest I'm not sure where either of them are. I suppose they're at home in a drawer but they're not at home alongside my All-Ireland football medal. No way.

Two years previously, I got upset on the pitch. This time I was more in shock. Neasa, of course, ran out and Ailbhe wanted to do likewise. It was nice to have family there but having to walk around the pitch without the cup and doing it for the last time and saying goodbye to the Munster fans as captain was tough. Some of the lads couldn't do it. They were gutted and I was gutted, too.

It's hard to describe the feeling. This may sound a bit extreme and dramatic but it was like somebody died belonging to you. It cuts to the core of you, there was something that you wanted so badly and all of a sudden it was gone and there was no way of getting it back. That's like death, really. It's not as bad, obviously, but there's no comeback. O.K., it was only a rugby match but it was also a job and a life long ambition and your whole life revolves around it.

The supporters were great again. There was nothing negative, no ill feeling. We felt so badly for everybody. There was a reception after the game and it was hard to get anybody into good form. I can laugh at it now but it was like a wake. We saw the Leicester people heading off on their short journey home with the cup and we were on the way to Cardiff Airport with nothing and the total disaster unfolding there. The crowds let us jump the queue into the departure area but meeting the people made it even tougher. There were big crowds at Shannon as well and it was almost embarrassing because we felt we had let them down again. I'd say for the first time ever, I didn't have a drink after a match. I might have had a bottle of Heineken but it did nothing for me. I felt if I began drinking, I'd get even more depressed so the whole Galwey family went off to bed not long after arriving at Jurys in Limerick.

Later on the Sunday we had a drink or two in Claw's (Peter Clohessy) but I just couldn't get into the buzz of it so we went back to Kilkenny. I was meant to meet John Keane, the son of John B., (the playwright) who was coming through Rosslare from the match. But he rang me to say that his father was sick and he had to head for Listowel instead. That made me think, hold on now a minute, here we are complaining about losing a match and this fella is probably going home to bury his father. That was the reality of it and it woke me up a bit. John B. did pass away shortly afterwards, he was a great Kerry man and a very loveable person.

A lot of my friends from Kilkenny had gone over and were coming back on a bus from Rosslare, lads from the Tholsel, a rugby bar known as Benjys that would be my local along with Langtons. We have great support in Kilkenny in spite of it being such a hurling hotbed. It's amazing the number of people who go to the matches including Gus Tobin, a neighbour of mine from down the road who is originally from Waterford. He comes to me every morning after the matches and it's really like living in Limerick.

Anyway, this great big bus pulls up outside the house and of course the two girls loved that and had to get on board and enjoyed the novelty. Then the lads and myself headed for the pub and it was just what I needed. We had a few pints, I needed to get out of myself and it was like a breath of fresh air. The match was on the television and they asked if I wanted it turned off and I said no, it was something I had to get through, to see the match and the incident. The lads claimed the few days out were better than any All-Ireland and that made it easier.

Declan Kidney calls it an emotional rollercoaster and that's exactly what it is. You've great times, you have bad times. You experience all the emotions. You have fear, you feel very emotional, these are the things you experience as a professional rugby player, coming up against good teams and beating them for there's nothing like winning.

Irrespective of where we play in Europe, leading Munster out at Thomond Park is my greatest thrill, my proudest moment as captain. All of a sudden the crowd lifts you and if you're anyway iffy about the match, they give you that certainty that you'll do it, that they're behind you, and if you're struggling, we'll be behind you. Some of the wins we've had at Thomond Park over teams like Saracens, Stade Francais, Biarritz, Harlequins and all the rest, that's what playing for Munster is all about. It's huge. Every time we go out in a competitive match, everybody wants to give a hundred per cent. That's the legacy we inherited and while I suppose we will never be as famous as the team that beat the All Blacks, I still think we now have a better Munster team than we ever had.

Me in my first year

Family group at Eileen's Confirmation. My mother Bridget, Bishop Eamon Casey, my sisters Eileen and Mary, my father Freddie and my sister Frances, I'm in the front.

I TURNED MY HEAD AND MY DINNER WAS GONE!

I WAS born in St Catherine's Hospital, Tralee, now the home of Kerry County Council.

I am the youngest of a family of eight. My mother Bridget was first married to Paddy O'Connor with whom she had two girls and two boys. He died and she married Freddie Galwey. He was from Gortshanafa which is between Currow and Farranfore and he was a blacksmith in Currow. He used to shoe horses and make gates. He was a very talented man. He used to do a lot of things, fix machinery and the like. Our house in Currow is next to the church and we had a forge next to that, and it was a focal point for the people of the village and surrounding areas. A lot of people used to come there and it was great fun. I remember holding horses for my father when he was shoeing them. They were the farmers' horses. The big treat for me was that any horse who was shoed in my father's forge, I used to get a ride on the horse down the road, a few hundred yards or so.

My brothers were that little bit older. Thomas played rugby with Castleisland and Patrick won All-Ireland football medals at vocational schools level. Currow itself hardly sounded the kind of place where they would know much if anything about rugby. It was, understandably enough, a hotbed of Gaelic Football. However, it wasn't quite like that where the Galwey clan was concerned.

Rugby was in my blood because my uncle Mick was banned from football under the foreign games rule and took up rugby instead. They had a very good team in Castleisland at the time, including famous characters like Mick Doyle, Con Houlihan and John B. Keane. Con and Mick Doyle and I think John B played in the back-row and my uncle was in the centre. My uncle Mick Galwey won a minor All-Ireland medal with Kerry in the early fifties so the rugby would have come in the very late fifties and early sixties. My dad played a bit of football but spent most of his time away from home. As a youngster the tradition was that he would go away working on farms and eventually he became a blacksmith and we had a bit of a farm at home as well. We had about fifteen acres and rented another few as well and we all had to work on the farm, we had cows, pigs and so on.

There were ten of us in all and although you might never think it today, I was the smallest man at the table. I suppose I was a spoiled child alright with all those sisters looking after me. At dinner time, I would sit in between my mother and father with my hand over the plate. You'd be sent out to the back kitchen to get milk and your dinner would be gone when you came back. So you had to be cute like that. But we had a very happy childhood.

I went to Ranalough National School in Currow. Moss Keane and his brothers and the Doyles all went there. None of us will ever forget the day when the legendary Mick O'Connell came to our village. It was 1974 and we were all at a very impressionable age. It was a game between Currow and Valentia and we all got the autographs and got to speak to him. Only Kerry people really understand the significance of such an occasion. Micky Ned (Micky O'Sullivan) got engaged to a neighbour, Marian King, in 1975, the year he captained Kerry to win the All-Ireland and our school in Currow was one of the first in the county to see the Sam Maguire. It was my first time to get my hands on the famous trophy. My mother had a shop in Currow, sweets and fags, that kind of thing. She is Bridget Galwey, nee Herlihy, from Ballymacadam from just outside Castleisland. She knew everybody and to this day she remembers everybody. I remember the first thing I ever won. It was for musical chairs up in the hall. It was a little plastic poodle and a glass case over it and she has it to this day and that's very nice.

Love of family and pride in where I came from burned indelibly in the heart of Mick Galwey. I accept people at face value and adopt a policy of "fool me once, shame on you, fool me twice, shame on me". It was inevitable that a young man growing up in such a strong footballing environment would become involved with the local club from his earliest days. I wasn't particularly big for my age but I was soon challenging for places in teams containing lads several years older than myself.

My first game for Currow was in goal for the under twelves at the age of nine. I was very small at that time. I went through two growing periods. I got my tonsils out at the age of eight and I shot up after that. Well, a little bit anyway. When I was fourteen, I really shot up that summer, I remember going back to school in Castleisland and fellows couldn't believe how I had grown during the holidays. I suppose I continued to develop from then until I was 21 or so. When I was younger, because of the tonsils and the tonsilitis, I was always getting 'flus and my mother feared I was very frail, that I was a weak child, and that I would never grow. She thought I had little girls' hands on me.

The following year, I started playing wing-back, I was fairly quick at the time. We were beaten in a few finals. Currow is slap in the middle of Kerry and we were playing in the Castleisland and District competitions against the likes of Castleisland Desmonds, Brosna, Cordal, Scartaglen, Knocknagoshel and Ballymac, teams from around our area. I'm not sure if we won anything at under twelves but we had a good team. We won a county league at under 14, that was the first of the big time as far as I was concerned. By now I had gone from goal, wing-back, centre-back to midfield. As I was getting older, I was getting better, taking all the frees and so on.

It was a great time and place to grow up for any youngster. I had many good friends. My cousin, Tim Galwey, was just one. The Walshes, (Brendan was my best man many years later), Liam and Robert; a near neighbour, Mike Egan; Johnny Roche down the road. Great guys, great times. Currow is a big parish, it's actually Killeentierna Parish. Currow and Currans are the two main villages.

If you ever went on the train from Farranfore to Tralee, you'd go over Currans, it's only a small place. Currow was the capital of the parish, if you like. For some reason, there seemed to be a lot of boys around my age at that time. Mike Egan was born a week or two before me, Johnny Roche was born somewhere in between, and then there were Timmy Butler and Michael King who died shortly after birth. For some reason, five boys were born in Currow within a few months of one another and we subsequently became great friends. These were the fellows I grew up with. We all went on to play under 14, 16, 18 football for Currow and later to play rugby for Castleisland.

Rugby wasn't an issue with me then, I didn't play the game until 1983. I attended the Vocational School in Castleisland and I played a lot of basketball and liked it. I played with Currow and a team in Castleisland. I was handy enough. There was a team in Killarney, St Vincent's, and they asked me to go in and I did so for a while and I liked it but thumbing to Killarney on a cold winter's night wasn't a nice thought. So I played locally and would you believe, I also had a go at soccer and I liked that, too, but there was a shortage of pitches and the club fell through.

In any event, Gaelic Football had become my passion and my burning ambition was to turn out for the Kerry minors.

I have turned referee at a charity football game in Killarney in 1994. Mickey O'Sullivan the 1975 Captain of Kerry shakes hands with the legendary Mick O'Connell.

The Currow minor football team of 1983, that's me with the hair at the back.

Myself with Tima and John Browne

My first Cap for Munster U18's, played at the Railway Union Grounds in Dublin.

The Currow Trio, Moss Keane, Mick Doyle and myself pictured at the Brown Flesk River in Currow.

THE GREEN AND GOLD OF KERRY

IT WAS 1983 and I failed to make the Kerry minor panel. I remember a night when Currow met and beat Castleisland Desmonds in a county league division two final. Kerry were playing Cork a few days later and even though I got a few trials, I didn't make the squad. In 1984, however, and at the age of 17, I wasn't leaving anything to chance. It didn't help to be born in the month of October, which isn't good when you have ambitions to make a name for yourself in minor football, and by then, too, I had sampled and liked the game of rugby!

I loved it. My first ever training session was on a Friday night with Castleisland. They were heading off for a trial game the following day in Bruff. John Browne who I met for the first time asked would I come along and I said I would. John brought me all the way in rugby. Were it not for him, I can honestly say that I might never have had those vital early opportunities in rugby. As well as being President of Castleisland R.F.C, he was also the driving force behind the club. Subsequently, he became my source of encouragement and he followed me from Castleisland to Shannon to Munster and later Ireland. He and his wife Tima spent most of their weekends driving me to the various matches. At this time I had never played a match, just one training session, and ended up playing a Munster Youths trial down in Bruff. It was the first year of the Youths Intepros. It was a kind of a West Limerick team, there were fellows there from Abbeyfeale, Newcastle West, Castleisland, Bruff I suppose, and we were playing the city boys.

It was a tough experience. They put me in the second-row, probably because I was from Currow like Moss Keane. I did a few unorthodox things, appeared out in the middle of the field, made a few runs with the ball. They noticed me. I actually made a final trial but I was coming up against fellows who had been playing rugby all their lives and that told against me. However, I had a taste for the game now and although I didn't get into the side, at least I reached the final trial.

By then, I was regularly playing three matches in a week-end, a football match on a Saturday evening, a soccer match on Sunday afternoon and a rugby match on Sunday evening. I even remember playing three matches on the same day and it wasn't a bother.

The fun of rugby really got to me. I loved meeting up in Castleisland on the morning, driving off and stopping for burgers and chips on the way to the match, the game itself, and the few pints afterwards.

I used to try and cod the parents about the pints. But it was great. We used to come down to Limerick to play Shannon, Thomond, St Marys. God, they were tough games. I remember one time a friend of mine called Mike Egan came along. We told him this rugby was great craic and we were off to Limerick for the day and we roped him in for his first game - as a prop. He was propping against "Porky" from St Marys, a small, tough little fellow who knew what scrummaging was all about. I'll never forget it. You hear about props lifting fellows. Mike hadn't a clue what he was doing. So Porky lifts him straight up off the ground but if he did, Mike started kicking him into the knees, he didn't know what was going on. I was playing number eight that day and the tears were flowing out of my eyes with laughter. We had fellows like that and we had great stories.

At that time, it was a bad road from Kerry to Limerick, there was no Rathkeale by-pass or anything like that. We used to have to go through Croagh. When I started coming to Limerick first, the journey was an hour and a half, now it's an hour.

The delights of rugby, however, hadn't diverted me from achieving my ambition of turning out for the Kerry minors. Currow reached two division one finals and although they lost both to a powerful Dr Crokes side, I had laid my claim to a place in the county side.

We went on to win the Minor County Championship with a divisional team called Castleisland, an amalgamation of the entire district. My cousin, Tim, was captain and that was huge for all concerned. My first game for Kerry was against Limerick in Tarbert. I will always remember that day. As I left home, my father shook my hand and wished me well. It was as if we were moving on to new territory. His youngest child was now old enough to represent Kerry and it was a very proud moment for him. I remember Len Dinneen and Dan Larkin were playing against us, they had a good side and they nearly beat us. We were in Tarbert when the news came through the same evening that Cork had been beaten by Tipperary. It was the first time this had happened. We went to Dungarvan and beat Waterford - that was an occasion to savour. We went down there in a bus. When you're a young fellow from Currow, that's a big day out. I knew every inch of Kerry because I played football on every pitch in the county. But going to Limerick, Waterford, that was different. I remember going on a school tour to Limerick and going to the Crescent Shopping Centre. That was a fantastic school tour for us.

Then came the minor final of '84 and horror of horrors, Tipperary beat us. They had Brian Burke in their team, he was a fine footballer. Stephen Stack was on our side and there were three Currow fellows, Tommy Brosnihan, my cousin Tim and myself. In fairness, Tipp had a very good squad that year but losing to them didn't go down too well back home. Quite simply, Kerry weren't supposed to lose a football match to anybody and certainly not Tipperary. Still, just to play for the Kerry minors was a big thing and to an impressionable young mind, getting free boots and a bag and adidas togs was mighty. But the adidas business was bad news for the county board. It was the start of the Kerry hassle with adidas. We didn't give a damn, all we wanted was to be a part of it. It was the centenary year and Dublin beat Tipp. I remember being at the match and Kerry were playing the senior final and they beat Dublin.

By now, school was over for me. I started working for Charlie Nelligan, the renowned Kerry goalkeeper, in Castleisland.

I'm playing with the Kerry Team.

Training in Killarney, Connie Murphy, myself, Tommy Doyle & Jack O'Shea.

A QUALIFIED BAKER!

I COMPLETED my leaving certificate in 1983 and a year later discovered the joys and sorrows of living in Currow and serving my time as a baker in Castleisland four miles away - when my trusty bicycle was the only mode of transport.

I had enough of school, I didn't want to go on to college or anything like that. It was great fun working with Charlie Nelligan. The great Kerry goalkeeper. Sometimes you started at 5 o'clock and my transport was my bike. It was only four miles but in the morning at that time ... I often remember being out on a Friday night and going straight into work. You'd go out again on the Saturday night and fall asleep in the night club, no good to anybody. I was a qualified baker, I spent five years with Charlie. There was himself, myself and a couple of girls, you had to do everything, I got the hang of it and it was great.

Working with Charlie, you'd meet all the Kerry footballers. Any of them passing would call in to see him as essentially anybody leaving Kerry has to pass through Castleisland. There I was a young fellow and meeting Jack O'Shea, Paudie O'Shea, the Bomber and the other legends of our young world. The word would get around town - Jacko is in Nelligan's shop or so-and-so is in the shop and they really were awe inspiring guys for Kerry youngsters to be around. I remember playing in that Munster minor final of '84 and being very disappointed and a few of them said, to me, well done, you played well. And they actually knew my name, that was probably due to working with Charlie more than anything else, but it was still something that made you feel really good. 'Twas a scorching day in Killarney. Ambrose O'Donovan was captain of the senior team and that was the start of the second three-in-a-row and football in Kerry was absolutely huge.

Looking back further into growing up .... Kerry won an All-Ireland in '78 and we went to a neighbour's house to see it on colour television. I never saw my father so excited, Kerry scored five goals and the Bomber got three and there was Mikey's Sheehy's free on Paddy Cullen and it took over the county. That was about a month before Munster beat the

All Blacks. People ask me where I was that day and to be honest, I'm not too sure, probably down in Kerry practising Mikey Sheehy's frees and scoring goals or something like that. And I didn't give a damn about the rugby match although I do remember hearing the result. My cousin Brendan went to see it and obviously with Moss playing, the word came through that Munster had beaten the All Blacks.

I first saw Kerry play at the opening of Pairc Ui Caoimh in 1976. It was a draw and Kerry won the re-play. I best remember the All-Ireland victory in 1975 and having John Egan's crucial goal described to me by my brother. My father took ill with cancer in 1984 and it didn't register with me. Freddie Galwey was a very strong individual, a blacksmith, not the tallest of men and his youngest son believed he was indestructible. In a way, I was in denial. I believed my dad was simply sick.

I remember Stephens Day in '84, he was lying down and for the first time it struck me, Jesus, he is in trouble, wheezing and not feeling well. He deteriorated after that and died on January 17th 1985. The day he died I went to work as usual. My brother Patrick came down and collected me early. I got home at 1:00 to find everybody sitting around his sick bed. I knew when I caught his hand that he was aware of my presence and shortly after that he died. I was 18 and he was 48. At the time I tried my best to put it behind me but not a day passes that I don't think of him. Fate dealt him a cruel blow - he missed weddings, grandchildren and sporting moments any father would have been proud of. It came as a huge shock to me. At this stage, I was playing rugby with Castleisland and lucky to have it to help me get over the shock. The day he was buried was the day Ireland were meant to play England at Lansdowne Road and the game was postponed because of the snow and the frost.

The morning of the Triple Crown decider, I pulled on a red jersey for the first time. The Munster Youths played Ulster at the Railway Union grounds in Dublin, it's funny the things you remember, you recall the first one and forget hundreds that happened in the meantime. I was down in Cork last year and a fellow gave me a photo of myself and a few lads after that game, we're as country looking and as innocent looking as you'll ever see but it's a lovely photo, five of us sitting down after the match and we're very happy looking. We beat Ulster, looking back, it was one of the few times we did, little did I realise they'd give us many a hammering after that. We wore our club socks and there were two others from Castleisland on that side, Mike Cronin and Peter Browne. It was a great day for the Castleisland club and Peter, Mike and myself subsequently went on to win Munster Cup medals with Shannon.

My first time seeing an International had been the year before when Castleisland went to Dublin on tour. We went up on a Friday night and home on a Sunday. This was huge. This is what got me into rugby. This was a TOUR! For me at the time, it was the equivalent of going off to Argentina. In fairness the GAA showed me every corner of Kerry and Currow were very good to me and I'd never have a bad word to say against them. But this was Castleisland and they brought me to Limerick and Cork and other places for the first time. Now we were in Dublin and it was big time. It was my first International and Moss Keane's last for Ireland. We were on the South terrace and I loved looking down at Moss and the game and even though we got a hammering that day from a good Scottish team that went on to win the Triple Crown, it was a very special feeling.

What a week-end. Castleisland people living in Dublin put us up and I think we slept on floors, but nobody minded. We didn't have beds but we were in Dublin and out all night. Now I had been to Croke Park and Lansdowne Road. Going home, there was a bit of messing, a bit of scrummaging and a few line-outs and that, and somebody kicked out the back window of the bus. It wasn't Mick Galwey although I was back there alright. We were meant to be stopping off in the Shannon pavilion on the way home but because the back window was gone, the driver got a bit grumpy and we had to go home directly. It was getting a bit chilly as we arrived in Kerry! John Browne was the man who brought us to these games and it was an annual event. The following year, we all went along to the Shelbourne Hotel on Stephens Green and saw the Triple Crown winners coming out and we got a few autographs. That year, too, Castleisland bought their own ground, the Crageens, a big day in the club's history.

Rugby, as we are seeing, was beginning to play an ever increasing part in my young life.

SHANNON SENIOR TE

(Left to Right, back row): L. Guerin, Asst. Treasurer; R. Kean T. Healy; G. McLoughlin; M. Galway; N. O'Shea; N. O'Donov Gallagher, Selector. (Seated): M. Ryan, Secretary; M. McLou O'Brien, President; N. Glynn, Vice-Captain; S. Minihan; O'Hanrahan; T. Fitzgerald; P. Mc

EL — SEASON 1985/'86

Secretary; T. O'Sullivan; T. Heffernan; N. Cowhey; P. Healy; oylett; R. Irwin; G. Murphy; P. Carroll; F. O'Flynn, Selector; F. am Secretary; A. Moloney; J. Willis; G. McMahon, Captain; B. ; D. O'Sullivan, Coach; D. Gilligan, Treasurer. (Front): S. ; O. Kiely; J. Pierce; K. Flannery.

Ginger McLoughlin

A PINT WITH GINGER!

IT WAS 1985 and Munster were meeting the Australian Schoolboys at Thomond Park. It seemed as good a reason as any for myself and a few pals to enjoy a day out in Limerick. Contacts I made on that occasion were to play a major part in my future.

I remember being in the Shannon clubhouse after the match and Ginger McLoughlin bought me a pint. That was a big moment in itself - and I don't just mean the buying of the pint! John Brown said to me - hold on to the glass, that's unbelievable - but I didn't as it turned out because somebody else stood me another pint. This was my introduction to Shannon, the first time I had met the senior players although I might have played one or two under age games for them.

But I was still into Castleisland in a big way. One day I went down to Cork with the Castleisland senior team for a Minor C final at 12 o'clock in the morning. This, of course, was another big bus trip. We lost the match - and then we had to drive to Thomond Park for a North Munster under 18 league final against Young Munsters, I think there were about eight of us involved in both teams which was ridiculous, of course. Our trouble was that one or two fellows got injured and one or two others emigrated and we had just twenty players.

So in desperation somebody decided to play an illegal player, a schools player, Conor Slattery, he captained Rockwell the same year to win the Munster Schools Senior Cup and he later played with Cork Con. Pupils at rugby playing schools weren't eligible in this competition. His brother Barry worked in the bank in Castleisland and Conor had been down a few times but that didn't entitle him to play in a North Munster final for us! We put him in the Kerry socks and togs and a big bandage around his head to disguise him and gave him a fictitious name. But it didn't work, the Young Munster fellows were too cute. It was Jimmy Clancy who spotted him. Coming off the field, Jimmy was roaring at him - you lifted a cup with Rockwell a few weeks ago. It was a draw, 6-all, but we were disqualified and our boast was that even though we never won anything, we were never beaten. It was felt that playing Conor was something we had to do but I suppose we picked the wrong man, he was too well-known.

I remember a few weeks later, Young Munsters rang me and asked if I would play an under 20 Cup match for them but I said no because they were after objecting to us. Anyway, had I done so, it wouldn't have gone down well in Castleisland, I can tell you that. The system was wrong, having to play two finals in the one day was unfair. It was daft - Castleisland were in South Munster as seniors and in North Munster at under-age. Crazy, wasn't it, the first time I ever played in Musgrave Park, I played for the first time in Thomond Park the same day. Little did I realise that Thomond and Musgrave Parks were where I would earn my bread and butter twelve or fourteen years later.

At this point, something of a tug-o'-war broke out between rugby on the one hand and football on the other. Both wanted me strictly to themselves! My reputation as a rugby player was growing but I was already established in Kerry as a footballer having represented the county minors. In 1985, I graduated to the Kerry under 21 team under Mick O'Dwyer with another Castleisland man, Dermot Hanafin, and we had a well fancied panel. But we went to Cooraclare and lost to Clare and I wondered if there was a jinx on me after being on Kerry football teams beaten by Tipperary and Clare. This was not supposed to happen!

In fairness, Clare had a good team and a lot of them went on to beat Kerry in the Munster final in '92. At the end of '85, I was called up for a Munster under 20 rugby trial. All of a sudden, I was up against all these fellows coming out of schools, internationals and that, but I got on the team. I was the only one who hadn't been to a rugby playing school or wasn't playing for a senior club. That was a big step up but the conflict is very much there, I'm a Kerry under 21 and a Munster under 20. I'm playing with the Castleisland rugby team rather than the Currow footballers and in no uncertain terms being told there is an obligation to play for Currow.

But I was getting a lot of backing from Castleisland, being on the Munster under 20's was big stuff. We lost to Ulster above in Ravenhill and to Leinster in Musgrave Park, but it was good experience. In the middle of all that, I played a senior match for Bohemians. Eamonn Tobin was manager of the Munster team and he was cute enough, I suppose, he said - you need the experience, come down and play a senior match for Bohs. It was against Garryowen and it was my first senior appearance. I had played a few under 20 matches for Shannon by this stage and I remember a highly indignant Colm Tucker coming straight into the dressingroom after that game and asking what the hell I was doing with Bohs. It was only a once-off thing, I hadn't signed my life away to Bohs.

It was then that Shannon came after me in earnest. My first senior game was at number eight against Athlone. The Shannon team then was built around Niall O'Donovan and Sonny Kiely, so I was subbing mainly. Then I played against Greystones in Greystones and Tony Ward was in their side. I remember a game against Old Wesley at Thomond Park and Phil Orr was about to get his 50th cap and he was scrummaging against Ginger and this was my first sign of the competitive side of the game. Like all good props, Ginger put the pressure on in front of the stand, he still had something to prove and wasn't going to make it easy for a man getting his 50th cap.

Come the cup campaign and the captain Ger McMahon was injured and I got on for the semi-final against Bohs and we won that and went on to beat Garryowen in the final and suddenly there I was with a Munster Senior Cup medal. It was 1986 and though I went back to the football, I didn't get on the Kerry 21s because of my rugby involvement. Then came a bit of a strike with the Kerry senior team, something to do with the Bendix washing machines, and there was the opening of a pitch up in Tourmakeady in Co Mayo and Kerry couldn't get a team together. They couldn't be seen to be sending up the senior players because there was a strike going on. They rang Charlie Nelligan to know if he would play and he said no but there's a man here who will.

So I went up there and marked Liam McHale and did fine, wearing the rugby boots and all that, and afterwards they gave us an Aran jumper as a thank you for making the journey and we were delighted. Dwyer was obviously impressed with the way I played that day and he called me up for a challenge against Laois. By this time the strike was over, the big boys were back but I was still there.

1988; Sandwiched in between two Irish Forward Coaches, Willie Anderson and Niall O'Donovan.

1992; Philip Danaher hauls down Australian Tim Kelaher.

Three decades of playing for Munster

2000

2001

A famous venue, we played Wales in Wembley while their stadium was being built in February 1999. Peter and Anna Clohessy, Joan and myself and Philip Danaher.

The golfers - Keith Wood, John Langford, myself and Anthony Foley.

OGIE THE PROPHET!

I TRAVELLED to Portlaoise for that game in Charlie Nelligan's Granada in the company of Ogie Moran, Paudie O'Shea, Bomber Liston and Charlie himself. I was overawed by such company and didn't say a word, listening instead to all their stories and reminiscences of famous matches and great characters. Ogie changed the subject and started talking rugby, how great it was for me to have won a Munster Cup medal at the tender age of 19. And then came the words that were sweet music to a young man's ears and words I have never forgotten.

"You might be on the way to being the only man to win a Munster Cup medal and an All-Ireland football medal in the one year", said Ogie Moran, All-Ireland winning captain and a man destined to win eight of the most coveted titles in all of Irish sport. That registered with me.

Jaysus, he could be right, I thought, although I was still only a Joe Soap and not one of the big guys. I didn't get to play in Portlaoise but Mick O'Dwyer told me to come in training that week. That invitation said a lot and it stirred my blood. Could this be happening? Anyone could be brought along for a challenge match but this was Championship training. Serious stuff in Kerry. I was young and I was fit but I wasn't the finished article. I was 19. I trained with the Kerry team and it came to the first round of the Championship and I was among the subs. As luck would have it, I was asked to go the same day to a rugby coaching seminar in Rockwell. I was 22 or 23 among the Kerry subs, so I went to Mick O'Dwyer and told him the situation. He didn't make an issue of it and said - go off to Rockwell, you won't even be missed. People told me I was mad, I was on the Kerry panel and I was going to this rugby session and it wasn't even a match. I knew what they meant and feared they might be right.

Kerry won the same day. And it came to the Munster final against Cork in Killarney and Micko was true to his word and I was in the subs panel. Kerry won it in the end but weren't all that impressive. They struggled because they hadn't trained all out, they hadn't peaked and probably because of this, they were all really thrilled, they knew there was more gas in the tank. Dwyer said - now we've beaten Cork and there's much more in the lads. He probably took a gamble but that's the kind of guy he was. In the dressingroom, he said we're back in full training in a week's time and he announced that some guys had to come in early - Paudie O'Shea, the Bomber, Sean Walsh, Charlie, all the old experienced fellows - and myself. There was a cheer every time a name was called out and a special one when I was called, at last a young fellow, a new fellow.

The older lads knew the story, for me it was something new. The pounds used to roll off. We'd do fourteen laps of the goalposts, not of the field, it was aimed at endurance, knocking off the fat. It was great training and Dwyer ran the whole show, he was the man. Then you got on to the sharper stuff. They called it wire to wires, sprint over the far side, touch the wires and back again.

I was going well. At the time, it was a great Kerry team. Jacko and Ambrose were the midfielders, myself and Dermot Hannafin were the sub midfielders and I was able to cover for the forwards as well. All-Ireland semi-final day against Meath. They had beaten Dublin and they were a coming team. Ten minutes to the final whistle, Bomber twinges a hamstring. Dwyer gets up - Mick Galwey, Mick Galwey, get on the pitch. All-Ireland semi-final, 50, 000 people or whatever it was. I hadn't expected this and so didn't have too much time for butterflies. The Rose of Tralee was on at the time and so maybe there wouldn't have been that many Kerry people present. At the time, there was a tradition, or so it was said, that not too many people went to the semi-finals, that they'd wait for the final. Now they're happy to go to any match Kerry are playing.

Anyway, my mother, brother Thomas and sister Francis left the ground with ten minutes to go because they wanted to catch the train and they missed my involvement. I was on for the last ten minutes and I remember looking around the stadium and taking in the size of the crowd for the first time. Mick Lyons was their full-back and there I was marking him. He was kind of pushing me and I said - hey, you're pushing me but the next thing he gave me a dig in the ribs and Jaysus, he took the wind out of me, all the time with the ball down at the other end of the field. He gave me a right clatter and I was really heaving but I told myself - show no weakness. I was delighted to see the ball coming our way, otherwise I might have had to square up to him and I was a bit young and a bit green behind the ears for that.

I got the ball once. I gave it to Ger Power, he gave it to Mikey Sheehy and the goalie made a great save but at least I touched the ball, I was on the pitch, there I was playing at Croke Park. My only time. The excitement was terrific and I was elated. We went back home in the train and I was meeting all the supporters and suddenly they all knew who Mick Galwey was because he played senior for Kerry. To be respected in Kerry, you have to play for the senior team. Before getting on the train, we went to the Aisling Hotel at Hueston Station and I went straight into the bar and drank a pint. It was then I realised that none of the other players were drinking, that there was something wrong. They were serious sportsmen and if they drank their pints they wouldn't do it in public and certainly not in front of Mick O'Dwyer. I had the one pint and said that's enough, put that away, I was getting sheeps eyes from different places.

I trained away with the team in the build-up to the final and played a few matches with Currow. Working with Charlie, there was more hype than usual. The newspapers came and photographed Charlie and myself in our bakers hats and that kind of stuff. It was great gas. In training on the week of the final, I went over on my ankle and couldn't have played but in fairness to Mick O'Dwyer, he carried me along and told me not to mention it to anybody. He had plenty of back-up, Dermot Hannafin at midfield and Timmy Dowd was a sub as well. He came on and played a great game.

Kerry were behind against Tyrone that day but came back to win well. To go back on the training, it turned me from being a boy to a man. I was still slight but I had hardened up. You were training with all these stars. Their attitude stood out for me. They had a great will to win and they went through the pain barrier to do it. A lot of them had knocks and bruises and some were coming to the end of their careers but they did what they had to do. You had fellows getting sick at sessions. When that happened, there was always a great cheer. I never got sick but I was often on the verge of it the training was so tough. I can't say I ever felt like getting physically sick from the rugby training whatever about a night on the beer. 'Twas a sign of weakness if you got sick and that's what Dwyer was looking for, he was looking for talented fellows but he wanted to see a tough edge to them as well, a mental toughness is what he wanted and that's what he got. Look at any of his players, they were all mentally very tough.

After the game, I stood down at the bottom of the stand as they all went up to the top. I had an injured leg and of course I was young and a bit shy. If I had my time all over again, I'd probably have been up there alongside Tommy Doyle getting the cup. There was Tommy lifting the Sam Maguire. It was unbelievable, Kerry had won another All-Ireland and I was very much a part of it. We stayed that night in the Grand Hotel in Malahide. I well remember on the night before, we went down on the beach and it was there that Mick O'Dwyer gave his team talk. This was tradition but it was new to me. Fantastic. Everybody has a ritual before a game and this was something the Kerry teams did. Another was to attend Mass in the hotel on the Sunday morning. I really liked that.

Then, in the dressingroom beforehand, Paudie O'Shea brought the backs into the showers and they had their private team talk. In the training sessions, you had the backs and the forwards. The backs had this thing that the forwards were not going to score. It was tougher than any game. You often saw them come to blows, Tommy Doyle marking Pat Spillane and they swinging out of one another. Paudie O'Shea in the corner and he roaring out at fellows and this was carried out on to the pitch. This was the passion. Paudie pulled the backs together inside in the showers and you could hear the roaring and screaming inside from Paudie. This was what they were going to do and in fairness they did it.

Shouting is easy but unless you do the business, it's no good. I learned a lesson from that when I became a captain myself. It's easy to talk but you have to put the talk into words. It was their attitude, the way they prepared, it was totally professional and these were all fellows doing a day's work and who then went on to training. After the game, there was a big dinner and reception at the Grand Hotel in Malahide and there was one the following day in the Burlington. And then the escort to the station and coming down in the train. It was a huge thing coming home to Kerry with the Sam Maguire.

In Millstreet, there was a big crowd at the station, even though it was in Co Cork. They wanted to see the cup and the lads said to me, you bring out the cup, and I'd had a few pints and I did so. Mick O'Dwyer came out, too, and we showed it to a couple of nuns and we shook hands and they were thrilled. After that, it was on to Rathmore and Killarney and the big parade around the town. We got up on the back of Doyles trucks, that was the tradition, then the speeches, then on to the bus, on to Farranfore which would be the nearest place to Currow. There was a massive crowd there from Currow. Charlie, Tommy Doyle, Paudie O'Shea, myself and a few officers of the County Board got out. My name was mentioned in the speeches as the local boy and they presented me with a bottle of champagne, the first one I ever saw. Off it went with a pop and it was a great laugh. On from there to Tralee and a big crowd in Denny Street and a reception in Horans. It was all a bit of a fairy tale.

On the Monday night, we went down to Tommy Doyle's home town of Annascaul and going through Blennerville on our way, Tommy had to get on to a horse and trap to cross the bridge into West Kerry. People were asking me for my autograph and I felt part of the whole thing. In Annascaul, we were dancing polkas in the middle of the street and after that my ankle acted up for I had done the ligaments badly and the following day the doctor put me into a cast for three weeks and I was on crutches for that time.

A few days later again and I met Tommy Doyle in the street in Tralee. He asked what was the craic and I told him we were thinking of going to the races in Listowel. Jaysus, he says, do me a favour and bring out Sam Maguire for me and I said I will. So anyway he gave me the cup and there I was with the Sam Maguire in the middle of the day. So I brought it home to my mother and of course she was delighted to see it. Then I brought it to my grandmother who was still alive at the time and made a few other calls and they were all thrilled and amazed to see it coming in the door.

We drove off to Listowel races with the Sam Maguire and when we arrived at the gate, people saw we had the cup and they let us in and they told us to go where we liked. The guy with me was Billy O'Connell - a gas man who played prop for Castleisland - and I was on crutches so he carried the Sam Maguire and this woman saw us and said - aren't they fat enough to be part of the Kerry team - she thought Billy, a prop, was a member of Mick O'Dwyer's All-Ireland winning side. Memories are made of this.

And we had further reward in the tours that followed. Two trips. One was to New York by the Kerry County Board and the Supporters Club who raised money for the team through dog nights, bingo sessions, whatever. Out there, you were staying with Kerry families but I had brothers and sisters, Patrick, Mary, Eileen and Hannah, in New York and I was with them and that was fantastic. They're still there. After that, there was a match in Chicago. I couldn't play because of my ankle but I met a guy, Dave Cahill, who was originally from Currow and I stayed with him and he showed me a great time. The following year, the All Stars tour took place to Chicago and San Francisco and I was part of that, too. When you are only 19 or 20, that's some adventure.

1991; Kenny Hooks and Des Fitzgerald at the back, myself and Brian Rigney, the day before my first cap.

Playing with St. Kierans

County Champions St. Kierans 1988.

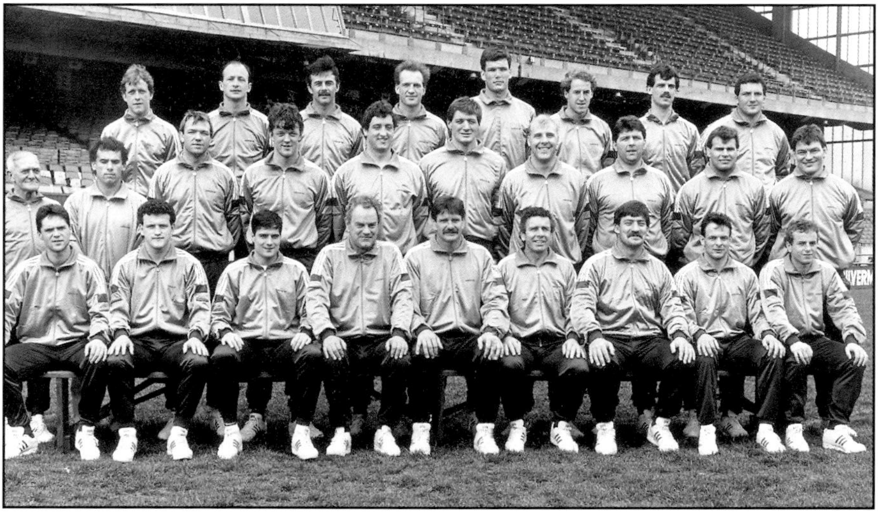

The Irish Squad which toured France in 1988, my first real taste of touring.

COUNTY CHAMPIONS!

I WON another Munster Cup medal with Shannon in 1987 and played football that summer. However unlike now, rugby finished at the end of April and ceased to exist for at least 4 months and I threw myself wholeheartedly into the Kerry U21 football campaing. The Munster final was a replay of the minor final three years previously as once again we were playing Tipperary. We drew with them in Tralee and the replay was on in Clonmel. It was a close thrilling match made more remarkable for the free for all which involved most of the 30 players. At this stage, comments like "You're not playing rugby now" and "Stick to the rugby" were common from the opposition, the sideline and even the odd referee. Funnily enough, I always took it as a compliment. We eventually beat Tipperary by a point after extra time. I scored a goal from midfield in the All-Ireland semi-final victory over Galway in Ennis. The final against Donegal in Tuam was a draw and we lost the re-play. A lot of that Donegal team went on to win an All-Ireland Senior Title a few years later. I remember it as being a great summer. I often meet some of that team at rugby matches - people like P.J. Gaire, Martin Downey, Stephen Stack and Gerard Murphy - and the conversation often goes back to the U21 title we left after us. At this stage Joan, my family and friends were following me around the country 12 months of the year to rugby and football matches. Kerry seniors were also beaten in the Munster final that year, I was back in the panel and played several challenge matches. Of even greater interest was my involvement with the Munster rugby team. I arrived on the scene at the same time as Peter Clohessy and we were members of the squad that travelled to Ravenhill, a venue that was to prove singularly unfruitful for the men in red, in the autumn of '87.

At the time, you got your Munster jersey, your socks and your togs but no tracksuit. I was a sub that day and there I was above in the middle of the Ravenhill stand in my Kerry tracksuit. It had to have been a first in that part of the world! We drew with Ulster 10-all and I also subbed for the next match against Leinster in Thomond Park. Tony Ward was playing for Leinster but Munster beat them. I met the Bomber, Sean Waslh and Ogie Moran going into the match, they came to watch in the hope that I would get a run. The thought that guys I had looked up to for so long would go to that sort of trouble gave me a very good feeling.

Anyway, there was a celebration in Killarney that night, a celebration of the golden years of Kerry football which basically meant that anybody who ever won an All-Ireland medal between 1975 and '86 was being presented with a lovely Waterford Crystal vase suitably inscribed. It was as if they knew the writing was on the wall at that stage, that the county wasn't going to have too many more golden years. There I am at the back of the picture with all the captains in the front row, probably more than fifty guys, the core being those who won eight All-Ireland medals. At this time I was working with John Browne of Kerry Keg. Part of the job was lifting beer kegs - great training.

I got on the Munster rugby team and Shannon went on to win the Munster Cup again. I remember we beat Cork Con in the semi-final on an awful day in Musgrave Park and we were all knackered after it. I had a shower, put on my clothes and drove down to Currow and played a semi-final of the Junior Championship that evening. Keen and fit and all as I was, I suppose I was beginning to wonder how long more I could combine the two games while trying to attain the highest standard in both. Then I was called up for the Irish Shamrocks tour to France, I was drafted in for Donal Spring and Nicky Barry came in for somebody else so we were the young guns out there. Tony Ward was on the trip and people often asked if I ever played in the same team as Wardy. I certainly did - and the last score he ever got in an Irish jersey was the conversion of my try against the French Barbarians.
John Browne of course made the trip and I was delighted to be able to give him my first Irish jersey - albeit a touring one. Another Shannon man and great friend of mine to make that trip was David Floyd. In the days when my mode of transport was my bike, David regularly made the return trip from Foynes to Shannon via Castleisland each way to take me to training with Shannon. That's real club loyalty. They both ended up travelling on the team bus as they were the only two supporters there. It made the trip extra special.

It was on that tour as well that they started calling me Gaillimh. Everybody had to have a nickname and Kenny Murphy I think it was who came up with Gaillimh. To most of us, it was pretty straightforward but it threw the northern lads a bit. To watch them trying to spell it was gas ... Willie Anderson would write down Golive and we'd all have a great laugh and he didn't understand why!

I came back from the rugby tour and played for the district side St Kierans, our senior divisional team. We struggled to beat Feale Rangers in the first round of the County Championship at Ballymacelligott. Then we played the Stacks in Tralee and I got a point in the last minute to force a draw and we brought them out to Ballymac and we beat them there. Then we played the Desmonds, this was seen as a local derby which would make the (Old Firm game) look like a stroll in the park, now you had fellows who grew up together playing against each other on opposite teams. We beat them in the semi-final and suddenly the hype was back in a big way. The county was buzzing - could these greenhorns from around Castleisland, playing as a unit in the championship for the first time, put one over on one of the long time aristocrats of Kerry football?

We were into the final against Dr Crokes of Killarney. But by the time this came around, the rugby season was back in swing. The Irish team were training and Munster had a match against London Counties on the Saturday of the county final. I subsequently learned that Munster didn't give caps for the game even though 'twas a fantastic London team so maybe I shouldn't have bothered. Anyway, I played against them up in Musgrave Park. The boys at home begged me not to play, if you get injured and that kind of thing, we'll be wrecked for tomorrow. But I said I have to play, it was my decision, here I was back from a tour of France with all the Irish gear. I was really gripped by the rugby.

I played for Munster and it didn't go down well with some die hards. To make matters worse, Jerry Murray came up to me after the game and said the Irish coach Jimmy Davidson wanted me in Dublin the following day for an Irish session. I told him I had to play in the county football final but he laughed and asked what he was going to tell Davidson, a man who wouldn't have too much interest in a gaelic football match at the other end of the island! It wouldn't have meant much to him and I understand that but in Kerry, you must be joking, it was one of the most important matters on any football man's agenda. Of course, I had to play the county final. It was huge in Currow and all over Kerry, there was so much speculation, so much passion and pride - if we were to win, we'd be legends in our own liftimes for heaven's sake! Trouble was, I was endangering my rugby future and once again the conflict between the two games had me bothered.

There was a chipper in Castleisland and after training they would give us chicken and chips and Ossie Bennett - father of Willie who now works with the Irish team - was down from Kilkenny to give us rubs and so on. John McNally, a Tyroneman originally and a teacher in Castleisland, pulled the whole thing together. He was a great coach. The effort made by everybody was enormous and we felt we just couldn't let the people down. Had I been injured in that rugby match and not able to play against Crokes, I shudder to think of what would have been said.

But I was o.k. and I went out and everything went well. We won it handy enough. St Kierans had won the county championship. We could hardly believe it, we had to pinch ourselves to be sure we weren't dreaming. There were several Currow men on the squad. Timmy Brosnan and myself were at midfield, Eamonn Walsh centre-back, Brendan Lane the goalie, Pat Dennehy, Mikey Brosnan, Tommy Hickey, Mossy Dore were all there. A few weeks later and Currow won the County Junior Championship. Another red letter day. It's difficult to explain to people outside of Kerry just what it all meant and, boy, did we celebrate!

Winning the county title with St Kierans meant I was Kerry captain in 1989 and I led the side out against Limerick at Askeaton. We won but I was dropped for the Munster final which Kerry lost to Cork who in turn went on to win the All-Ireland. Playing so many tough matches was now getting to me and I decided I would give preference to rugby from then on. I played a few games afterwards with Currow, including an O'Donohue Cup Final which we lost by a point to Dr. Crokes in Killarney. I flew from London on the day of the match where Munster played London Irish. Subsequently Currow went on to win the O'Donoghue Cup a few years later and they slagged me that if I was not around they would have won a few more. We won a couple of East Kerry titles but essentially that was it.

Munster Pack, Niall O'Donovan, Colm Tucker, Ralph Keyes, Philip Danaher with me in the rear.

In the lineout for Munster with Donal Lenihan and All Black Zin Zan Brooke.

PLAYING FOR IRELAND

FROM THE day I was born until 1986, I was Mike Galwey. I had an uncle Mick in Currow and you couldn't have two Mick Galweys in such a small community! I was even Mikey to some and only my mother called me Michael. All that changed when I came to Limerick. I was introduced as Mike Galwey but there aren't too many Mikes around Limerick so I immediately became Mick and that's the way it's been ever since.

Shannon and Munster quickly took over my sporting priorities. The three-in-a-row Munster Cup successes of 1986, '87 and '88 paved the way for my arrival as a Munster regular from 1987 onward. I made my first appearance in the red jersey against Connacht and that, combined with good performances for Shannon in the cup, earned me a place in the Irish party that performed so creditably in France.

At the time there was a trip to Padova in Italy with Munster to prepare for the visit of the All Blacks in 1989. It was the first time the New Zealanders had played Munster since the famous game in 1978 and of course everybody wanted to be in the team. John Pearse and Sonny Kiely got their first Munster caps that day and we also had fellows like Brian Spillane and Paul Collins. The Interpros. were also very big that year because the four provinces were playing the All Blacks and we all wanted to do well. I remember we had beaten Leinster and Connacht and then we had to go up to Ravenhill to meet Ulster and they beat us in the last ten minutes, something they were going to do to us for the next ten years and little did we realise it at the time.

The atmosphere in Cork for the All Blacks game was terrific, they had built special stands and all that, and we actually started very well. We gave them a soft try coming up to half time but it was a good game and much harder than anything I had encountered before then. They beat us fairly well in the end. A few lads picked up injuries and so I was called up to the Irish squad on stand-by for the following week's International against the New Zealanders along with Brian Robinson and Noel Mannion. We were there for the whole week-end and that was my first taste of the International scene. We were involved in the training and it was a good idea even though the others called us the C team because we weren't on the team or even the subs, we were just on stand-by. But it was a nice touch, one of the first times they brought the fringe players in to show them the ropes and give them a taste of the International atmosphere, we were put up in the hotel and all that and it was all new to me.

We were staying in the Westbury off Grafton St. What got to me was walking through the crowds, it was fantastic. You probably wouldn't get away with it now. There was the escort to the match, it was a great buzz, to be in the dressingroom before and after, there was pressure in that even though I wasn't playing and obviously it was something I got to like. It was the day that Willie Anderson and the Irish team stood up to the All Blacks when they were doing the haka.

That was the famous one but in actual fact Munster had done it the previous week at Musgrave Park. It was Pa's (Whelan, the Munster coach) idea to face them up. I'll always remember Buck Shelford, the two of us made eye contact, he was their captain and their main man and he had led them to the first World Cup. I started about ten yards away from him but he wound up stuck in my face. We stood our ground and they advanced. I just looked at him and wasn't going to look away very quickly and neither was he going to be intimidated but he just came towards me and if I was to be true to myself, I really was intimidated by it but at the same time it was an experience, it was something we did, we laid down the challenge to them. The following week got all the publicity and I suppose the All Blacks were ready for it. They were almost touching, if that had happened, the next thing there would have been a blow but it didn't come to that.

That was a great game. Ireland started very well and one of the All Blacks went down injured and somebody said and I think it might have been Mick Molloy, that it was a tactic, they were just trying to take the steam out of the Irish. Ireland fought bravely but the All-Blacks showed why they were world champions.

I was moving ever closer to a full Irish cap. I subbed against Wales at Lansdowne Road in 1990, a match Ireland won comfortably, and the following autumn I was a member of an Ireland B team that walloped Argentina, Federico Mendez, Hugo Porta and all, at Thomond Park. Simon Geoghegan was a member of the Irish side and scored a smashing try. I was a sub for the International a week later and perhaps I was better off because it was far from a convincing display, and I was very much in the forefront after a good game for the B team against Scotland in Belfast.

Between Christmas and the new year, 1991, we headed off for Portugal and warm weather training, the first time this had happened. We were doing track work and it was all new to me. I was in bits after it. Full time training was just coming in at the time and Fitzy (Ciaran Fitzgerald) was in charge. We had a kind of a final trial out there and the pitch was a joke, could have been a soccer pitch or something, 'twas inside a big wall, more like an old orchard that had been renovated. We came home and played a few more AIB League matches and then the team was announced and I was on it. There were a load of new caps, Simon Geoghegan, Rob Saunders, who was also captain; Gordon Hamilton, Brian Robinson and myself. On the Friday before the match, Neil Francis cried off and Brian Rigney was called up. Personally I was delighted that Brian was in. I had played with him in B matches and found him to be a hard-working reliable second row. The kind of fellow you want to partner you on your first cap. So in fact we had six new caps facing France at Lansdowne Road.

At the time, I was too excited to be worrying about that. One of the good things was that the team was selected two weeks before the match which gave you time to soak it all in. I remember how I heard the news. I was up in Kilkenny, Joan was living there at the time, and I had gone up after a match on Saturday and stayed until Monday morning. I was driving back to Castleisland for work with John Browne and was listening to the 10 o'clock news on Radio Two. They announced there were five new caps on the Irish team and my name was read out. I was about six or seven miles outside Clonmel; there were no mobile phones at the time so I stopped in Clonmel and rang Joan and my mother. There was great excitement when I got to Castleisland that night. Colm Tucker came down from Limerick and a big crowd of us had a good few pints in the Crown Hotel.

Two years previously, a piece appeared in what was then "The Cork Examiner" predicting that Mick Galwey was "about to follow in the illustrious footsteps of three other Currowmen, Mick and Tom Doyle, and Moss Keane, who have played for Ireland". My mother Bridget read the article at the time and commented that "it was a bit exaggerated". When contacted about her son's selection to face the French for his first cap, Mrs Galwey accepted she might have been something of a "Doubting Thomas" before going on: "Of course we are all very proud of Michael and what he has achieved and we are all looking forward to the big day. The Doyles lived only a hundred yards down the road from us and Moss Keane another mile or so. When the Internationals were on the telly, I would always be looking out for Moss and cheering him on. I suppose it was inevitable I would want Michael to follow in his footsteps".

Although the headline in the Cork Examiner screamed: "Rookie Captain and Five New Caps", I believe my selection was nearly expected at the time for I had played well for Munster and in the B matches but as it happened only one forward, Dessie Fitzgerald, held his place from the game against Argentina. The Saturday prior to the French match, I took the traditional rest before a first cap but travelled to Ballymena with Shannon for an AIB League game.

There was a buzz up there too for they had Brian Robinson winning his first cap and Stevie Smith was also in the Irish side. I met the great Syd Millar and Willie John McBride, probably for the first time. Millar gave me a bit of advice. Bob McConkey was standing there beside him when he wished me good luck and he assured me there will be no fear of you and that kind of thing. Then he said: 'forget about the ball for the first ten minutes' and it was probably a good piece of advice for at the time you had to fight your corner and a new cap might have been seen as something of a soft touch. I was marking this fellow Michael Tachdjian and he was a bit of a ruthless looking fellow. A few weeks previously he had done a bit of damage against Scotland. The first line-out was called on Brian Rigney and I just went across on the French guy and as I was doing so the elbow was coming across to meet me and there was a bit of a clash. Nothing major, but the marker was down and after ten minutes we were all so wrecked we started chasing the ball instead. Psychologically, you still have to fight your corner because rugby is such a physical game and it was probably more physical then. It was something that had to be done.

I was lucky to gain my first cap in the Five Nations at Lansdowne Road. Some guys are capped away on tour or whatever and that's fantastic for them but I wouldn't change anything that happened to me, playing France in the first match of the Five Nations at Lansdowne Road was the ideal situation for me. To run out in the green jersey to a huge roar and a massive Irish crowd is something that will live with me forever. In hindsight and now that I have 41 caps, I'm glad it worked out that way.

One of the guys playing that day against France was Brian Smith, Brian was a controversial choice especially because Ralph Keyes was on the bench and everybody believed he should have been the man. At the time there was Rugby After Dark and programmes like that on RTE and Smith's selection came in for a lot of criticism. I don't think the Irish supporters ever really warmed to him. He had a good running game and Ireland scored a lot of tries that year but Ralph Keyes was only a sub and when he came in for the World Cup later on that year he was the leading points scorer. Smith was O.K. as a person, he tried his best to be involved but a few weeks before the World Cup he headed off to Rugby League and the players felt disappointed, we had stood by him and probably felt a little let down by that but then Ralphy came in and did a fantastic job, probably a better one than Brian could have ever done.

Anyway, going back to the French match ... I remember a Shannon man Blondie Mac, Ger McNamara, he promised me a pint if I managed to tackle Serge Blanco, who was having his last game for France against Ireland. Blanco was a class act but I managed to get him and Blondie's pint was the thing I thought of straight away, it is not the kind of thing that should be going through your mind in the middle of an international game, but then everybody wanted to tackle Blanco, so I got my pint. The team was picked more or less en bloc for the next game against Wales in Cardiff. We drew 21-all and it was a great game. Jack Clarke got his first cap and scored a try. That was the day when we had seven backs none of whom were born in Ireland ... Jim Staples

(England); Jack Clarke (Kenya), David Curtis (Zimbabwe), Brendan Mullin (Israel), Simon Geoghegan (England); Brian Smith (Australia)and Rob Saunders (England), but in fairness, with the possible exception of Smith, they all had perfect Irish credentials and anyway the forwards were all Paddys!

We were running a lot of ball and it was good rugby if not good percentage rugby. To score 21 points was fine but to give away 21 was disappointing. After that game, I was dropped. I was shattered. I wasn't even subbing as Noel Mannion was covering the back five. In fairness to Ciaran Fitzgerald, he rang me on the Monday morning. He was headed for Killarney and gave me the news. He said to think about it and to ring him back if I wanted to have lunch. So we met in the Crown where five weeks earlier I had been celebrating the happiest time of my life, all of a sudden a month later and I'm out on my ear. There was a crowd around and when they saw me with Ciaran Fitzgerald, there was a bit of mumbling, he was seen as the fellow who dropped me. The word went through the town that Fitzy and Galwey were above in the Crown and all sorts of rumours started, things like Galwey is after giving it up, or he told Fitzy where to get off, or I was even after boxing his head off. In fairness to him, though, he talked to me, told me it was a close call and Neil Francis was a good line-out man. I felt hard done by but I stuck with it and then came the tour to Namibia.

We were basically training hard for the 1991 World Cup. The squad hadn't been finalised. There were four games out there and I came on as a sub in the second. My preparation wasn't the best because I wasn't officially on the subs bench for that game. Pako Fitzgerald, who was a bit down in himself having lost his place to Nick Popplewell, and myself, went into Windhoek on the morning of the game. Terry Kingston came along to do some last minute shopping. By this stage, Joan and I had decided to get engaged and with the help of the two experts, we chose a diamond which was later used for the ring. We got back to the hotel in good time to learn that Pat O'Hara had food poisoning and was out of the subs. I got the call to sit on the bench and came in during the game for Neil Francis as a partner for Donal Lenihan. Francis played with Brian Rigney in the first and Brian injured his knee and was out for a long time and then they flew Donal Lenihan out and he played in the second. It wasn't good news for me, essentially I was down to fourth choice second-row although I just had to keep the head down and as it turned out I was picked for the World Cup.

My first cap against France

IRELAND WORLD CUP SQUAD 1991

THE WORLD CUP 1991 - AND BEATING ENGLAND!

SELECTION ON the World Cup squad meant that I had moved up another rung on the second-row pecking order and gave me a feeling of great satisfaction. Outside of Munster, and sometimes within as we shall see, the consensus seemed to be that I lacked the height and consequently the line-out dynamism that was becoming ever more important in an evolving world game.

My admirers, however, argued that I more than compensated for whatever shortcomings might exist in the line-out with my wholehearted contribution in all other facets of the game. To be fair, various influential bodies and some pundits did seem to agree on the perceived line-out shortcomings and presumably why I was often asked to turn out at number eight and number six and that ultimately played a key role in my selection on the 1993 Lions touring party in New Zealand. Before that, however, there were even more pressing things to attend to - like a World Cup campaign and scoring a memorable try in a famous victory over England!

Our World Cup group was Scotland, Zimbabwe and Japan. We stayed out at Finnstown House and trained at Kings Hospital and were together for a week and going well entering the first game against Zimbabwe when Brian Robinson scored four tries and we put fifty points on them. I played the following game against Japan and even though they were physical and tough, we beat them well. I wasn't involved in the game over in Scotland, the infamous occasion when Findlay Calder took out Jim Staples and that led to a try and we were beaten. That was a very controversial game and it left a sour taste.

Anyway, we flew home and spent a few days recuperating in Parknasilla. We flew into Farranfore, home if you like for me, and we had good craic down there and did a bit of work on the GAA pitch in Sneem, played rounders and that kind of thing. Professionalism was just coming at the time. The players made a bit of a stance, it was more a storm in a teacup, there was never going to be a strike but it helped the players to pull together which was a good thing for it helped us on the pitch.

A bunch of us, Pako (John Fitzgerald), Eddie O'Sullivan, who was one of the fitness boys at the time, and others played golf at Killeen in Killarney, and we went to Pat Spillanes one night, and then it was back to Dublin and more training for the famous game with Australia. I wasn't involved and that was a big disappointment but Noel Mannion had been subbing all year. Pako and myself had to sit it out and indeed it was worse for Philip Danaher who was the only one of the 26 who didn't get to tog out at all.

After Gordon Hamilton's try, we were jumping all over the place and we thought we had done it. But they came back and in fairness got the winning try. All the talk afterwards I suppose was about Rob Saunders not kicking the ball into touch from the kick-off after Gordon's try; ironic isn't it because now they'd kill you for kicking to touch, it's all about keeping the ball alive. Then somebody said if we'd won that game it would have been the same as winning the World Cup for England. 'Twas a great adventure for me as I was still a young fella. I won't say it was my first tour because I had been to France and Namibia but it was the real thing, the first real big time stuff.

Having come so close to surprising the powerful Australians, who then went on to beat New Zealand in another Lansdowne Road thriller a week later and then England in the final at Twickenham, there was a great buzz for the game in Ireland in the aftermath of the World Cup. The players sensed it, too, and were determined to maintain the momentum once the 1992 Five Nations Championship came around. It was not to be. All four matches were lost but I gained additional experience with my inclusion for the last three matches of the campaign against England, Scotland and France. Five Limerick players, Mick Fitzgibbon, Paul Hogan, Mick Galwey, John "Pako" Fitzgerald and Richard Wallace played against France but unfortunately Ireland were heavily beaten.

After that, the prospect of a tour to New Zealand wasn't exactly very appealing. Several players didn't make themselves available and a new team was emerging. With Philip Danaher, my good friend, as captain, Michael Bradley also very influential and several other Munstermen like Pako Fitzgerald, Terry Kingston, Paul McCarthy and Mick Fitzgibbon at my side, I felt very much at ease - until we met the powerful Auckland provincial side a week before the first Test - and suffered a humiliating defeat. Eleven Aucklanders were in the All Blacks side and the country as a whole braced itself for the mother of all hidings in Dunedin.

They call the stadium there the house of pain and it certainly looked like we were going from the frying pan into the fire. We won the mid-week match and then there were a few surprises when the team was announced ...Paul McCarthy got his first cap, Terry was playing, also Poppy (Nick Popplewell); Paddy Johns and myself were in the second-row and Paddy only made the tour as a late call-up. Kelvin Leahy got his one and only cap that day at wing-forward and Mick Fitzgibbon was the other wing-forward. Mick played great rugby on that tour. He loved the New Zealand style and he did very well out there.

He was making some wicked tackles, in one game he put in twenty five tackles and being Mick, they'd be bone crushing tackles. But the New Zealanders were bigger, stronger men and he was getting hurt and he wasn't pulling back one bit. Eventually, his shoulders almost gave in. That first Test, we were on a hiding to nothing but we got off to a great start and Vinny Cunningham scored two tries in the first half, something no Irishman had ever done against New Zealand. Jim Staples got another. At one stage, we were leading 12-0 and we really got in among them.

The rucking game was something we really picked on over there. The first few games we were getting rucked off the field. Over there, you ruck everything out of the way and head for the ball. That's the one thing we learned that year, we had to, otherwise we were going to get hurt. We were rucking very well against New Zealand and everything was going well. Danaher started that game as captain and got injured and eventually had to go off and Michael Bradley took over. Kelvin broke his leg just before half time. Then, I tackled a fella and Mick Fitzgibbon was lining up to tackle another guy and next thing his boot came back and hit me straight into the nose and nearly ripped it off my face.
They were using Tuigamala a lot and towards the end Frank Bunce brought the ball up and gave a dummy and scored under the posts. They beat us 24-21 but I remember a Dungannon winger, Ronnie Carey,

he nearly intercepted a ball and it was bobbling, bobbling, bobbling and if he had held it we would have won but it slipped away ... there was war in New Zealand because they only beat us by three points. I remember Richard Loe was taken off and he didn't like that and he was dropped for the next match and they brought in Ollo Brown. We had given our all and a lot of us had to play a mid-week match against Manawatu. Even then, we led the All Blacks 6-0; we noticed that John Kirwan kept coming up so we put a ball in behind him and Neville Furlong got a try and Peter Russell converted. Neville played the game with a broken leg. They turned it around though and beat us heavily, it was one of those days when they were on fire.

As it turned out, it was a good tour, it hardened us all up and got us used to top-class rugby. After our break for the summer, it was time for the world champions Australia to come to Ireland. Munster-Australia was down for a Tuesday game. I had seen them play Leinster with their Test side the previous Saturday and they put out their second string against us but they were claiming that there was little between their firsts and seconds. We had injuries ourselves but it was a great team to be part of. There were four Young Munstermen and their influence was important. But Pako was dropped and they played Paul McCarthy at loose head and we all wondered how he would get on there but it worked out very well and we even got a pushover try.

There was a great buzz about the whole affair. Everybody wanted to see Australia because they were world champions and even if we weren't, let's say, as fashionable then as we are now, everybody wanted to see how Munster would get on against a touring side. It was an awful day and we started well. We got stuck in to them, upsetting them if you like. It was the last time we were totally negative against the opposition. It was also the last time it worked for us because we played them a few years afterwards and they gave us an awful hiding. We weren't the most skillful but we were 100% committed and it worked for us on the day.

They were at it as well and their wing-forward Sam Scott-Young took out Dan Larkin early on and he had to go off. There were niggly bits all the way and Peter Clohessy, of course, was flying around the place and they didn't like his style of scrummaging. Bob Dwyer made a big song and dance out of that subsequently. It was getting rough and I remember I was warned early on. Fellows were being tripped running across the pitch. If it was to happen to-day, you wouldn't get away with it. The French referee probably lost a bit of control and the crowd sensed we were doing well. Jim Galvin came on for Dan Larkin and was kicking the ball the length of the field and Philip Danaher and Brian Walsh were tackling like demons in the middle of the pitch. It was typical Munster passion, somebody puts in a tackle and three forwards hit the ruck and the ball comes out on our side.

It was a great game even though I got sent off after a bust-up at the end. Garrick Horgan, an Australian second-row, and myself wound up on the ground. Garrick, now playing with Harlequins was a big lad, a fair bit bigger than me, the two of us were handbagging I suppose for want of a better word, but the referee picked us out and sent us off. It was no big deal and we shook hands there and then. But a great story was told about Richie Wallace. He was looking for somebody to fight and the wallaby, their mascot, was on the ground nearby and he drew a kick at it. That was Richie's contribution. Then there was Ger Clohessy, he had been boxing and the bandage went down over his face and he couldn't see what he was doing so somebody nearly boxed the head off him. Australia weren't pulling back. Jim Galvin dropped the winning goal and 'twas a fantastic day for Munster because we had beaten the world champions. And then we got cocky and thought we knew it all and suddenly we were beaten by Ulster and Leinster.

Garrick Horgan and myself got four days suspension. After the game, he and I went down to Jurys together. Noel Murphy was there and gave a fantastic character reference. I didn't know what was going to happen. The game had been televised and I thought maybe they'll make an example of us. The expression I used to explain what happened was that I was a victim of circumstances. I was very pleased with that one wherever it came from. Benny O'Dowd, a recent past President of the Branch, chaired the meeting and it came to dishing out the suspension and the first thing I heard was four. I thought, oh Jaysus, four weeks or four months, but he then said days. That was great and we weren't complaining and during the night Garrick and I posed for photos and that was that.

After Munster beating them, there were hopes that Ireland would do the same to the Wallabies on the following Saturday week. But they walloped us and they were awesome on the day. Not long after that, I got a bit of a scare playing for Shannon up in the north. After tackling some guy, I felt a numbness in my arm and I was worried about it. The following day we had an Irish session and Mick Molloy sent me for an x-ray. The specialist had a look at it and immediately put me in a collar, one of those plastic ones that went halfway up my face. He gave me all the bad news first, that there was a shadow on my neck, I might need an operation, that I might be in a cast for ten weeks, that I might even need a graft off my hip on to my neck. The following day there was no change and word was getting out that I was in hospital and that my career might be over. And then on the Thursday, they came in and told me I was fine. Jaysus, it was some relief, for I was sure I'd never again play rugby. It was a brother of Colm O'Rourke, the Meath footballer, who gave me the good news. As it turned out, I went home on the Friday and played a match for Shannon on the Saturday so the show was back on the road but at the time it was really scary.

From thinking I was finished, I was picked as a sub against France in '93, Peter Clohessy's first cap. As it turned out, there were a few injuries and they turned to Pat O'Hara, Terry, myself, the Munster lads if you like.

We played well against France and it was a match we could and probably should have won. France got a late try to put the game out of Ireland's reach. But the feeling was that the corner had been turned, that the players were "hardening up". Eric Elwood was brought into the side and Ireland won in Cardiff against a Welsh side that had already shocked England! Gerry Murphy was coach by now and he and fifteen Irishmen were about to enjoy one of their finest hours. You would never have thought so in the build-up to the England match at Lansdowne Road on March 20th, 1993. The "Rothmans Rugby Union Yearbook" set the scene: "A trip to the bookmakers on O'Connell Street on Thursday left no doubt as to who was going to win. England were 6 to 1 on, there was only one team in it". The public at large seemed to agree but those who mattered most saw things differently.

England were going very well at the time. Even though Wales had

shocked them, they were still coming for the Championship. 'Twas the week-end the Lions team for New Zealand was due to be announced and obviously they were expecting everybody to click. They had all the old hands, Carling, Guscott, the lot. But as it turned out, we were pretty well up for it, playing with confidence, and 'twas a good time for Irish rugby. Looking back, the tour of New Zealand stood to us.
They got the first score and then Eric kicked a great penalty into the wind and at half time we were still level and turning to play with the elements. We kept them under pressure, rattled them, and Eric kicked a penalty and two dropped goals. 12-3 in front. England were obviously much bigger than us, enormous guys like Bayfield and Dooley, but we actually did well against them in the line-outs. Willie Anderson was the forwards coach and he had us hopping off the ground and he told us if we won five line-outs in the opposition half that we'd win the match as well. We did that and more and won two of their throws.

Then came the try. I remember Danaher put in a big tackle in the middle of the field. After that, there was a bit of a skirmish and at that stage the backs were playing very well, Ciaran Clarke, Simon Geoghegan, Richie, all these guys, were carrying great ball. We drove on and I was coming late to the ruck and Michael Bradley took a tackle, passed to me and I saw the line and, Jaysus, I couldn't believe it was there. I knew there was somebody on my back, it was Tony Underwood, and if you look at it in slow motion, I just barely made it, I was falling from about five yards out but I eventually got the touch down and it capped a great day.

My sister Mary flew all the way from New York on the morning of the match and was going back again the following morning. I didn't have a chance to meet her but left a ticket in the Berkeley Court where we were staying. But for some reason she couldn't get it and so she went out in the street and in fairness bought one at face value and that's why she was where she was when I scored the try - in the Kerry Corner, as Con Houlihan called it, because Tom Doyle and Moss Keane scored tries there as well.

To this day, Mary's embarrassed about it. 'Twas spontaneous. I scored a try. Everybody ran in on the pitch. She ran in as well, she couldn't get near me with the crowd and 'twas only when I was walking away that she ran after me and gave me a big kiss. I was kinda surprised to see her alright, but I just said, Jaysus Mary, how are you. Would you believe, with all the excitement I missed her that night and didn't meet her again for four months. The final whistle came shortly after the try and sure it was fantastic, the one and only time I was carried off shoulder high. We were in no rush off the pitch because we often went off it before and since with our heads between our legs. The people were great. Any day you beat England 17-3, especially at Lansdowne Road, is one to remember. We had a great night.

And then of course there was considerable speculation about the Lions team. I was involved with the Irish sevens squad at the time and we were in Dublin waiting to go out to Hong Kong for the sevens out there and I'll always remember most of the lads were there on the Monday morning at a meeting in Lansdowne Road when Noel Murphy came in holding a fax. The papers were saying we'd have seven Lions because we had beaten England and Wales and a lot of guys were being tipped. Anyway, Noel came in and said something like 'it's disappointing as far as I'm concerned and a lot of people in this room will be disappointed. We've only two Lions, Nick Popplewell and Mick Galwey'. When he said only two, I thought it was gone but I was obviously delighted with the news but so many others were disappointed. I went off to Hong Kong and played only three minutes of a game and had a great time. On my return from Hong Kong, the Currow Parish Council, in conjunction with the GAA Club, Basketball Club, the Cycling Club, the Youth Club and the Athletics Club, held a celebration in my honour. They put me up on the back of one of John Browne's trucks and paraded me through the bunting bedecked village led by the Cullen Pipe Band. Afterwards, we went to the parish hall for a reception. Moss Keane made the effort to come down. It was one of my earliest and toughest speeches for I was entirely shaken by the whole occasion. Mike O'Shea, our local tenor, sang late into the night on what was a memorable occasion in Currow. I was also on the World Cup sevens in Scotland where we did very well and that was my rather strange preparation for the Lions!

1991; Squad group in Parknasilla

BACK ROW: R. Jones, T. Underwood, K. S. Milne, P. H. Wright, R. Underwood MBE C. D. Morris, W. D. C. Carling OBE A. P. Burnell, A. Clement, N. Popplewell, S. Gibbs, J. Leonard.

CENTRE ROW: M. C. Teague, P. J. Winterbottom, B. B. Clarke, D. Richards, W. A. Dooley, M. C. Bayfield, A. I. Reed, D. F. Cronin, M. Galwey, J. C. Guscott, R. Webster, I. Hunter.

FRONT ROW: K. Murphy (Hon. Physiotherapist), C. R. Andrew, B. C. Moore, I. Evans, G. D. Cooke OBE (Hon. Manager), A. G. Hastings (Captain), I. R. McGeechan OBE (Hon Assistant Manager/Coach), R. F. Best (Hon Assist Coach), S. Hastings, S. Barnes, Dr. J. P. Robson (Hon. Doctor). INSET: V. J. G. Cunningham, R. Wallace, M. Johnson, A. D. Nicol.

LIFE WITH THE LIONS 1993

MY SELECTION was controversial, especially in Britain, because I was picked as a wing-forward. I owed my place primarily to my performances in the second-row while pointing out that I had played number eight against France earlier in the season and had done very well there. I felt the English couldn't give me too hard a time because they had a sixteen-strong representation themselves! Not that you could argue about the inclusion of players of the calibre of Rory and Tony Underwood, Will Carling, Jeremy Guscott, Rob Andrew, Jason Leonard, Wade Dooley, Martin Bayfield and Dean Richards. To balance matters, the party was captained by the great Scottish full-back Gavin Hastings, with another Scot, Ian McGeechan as coach although the management team was led by a couple of other Englishmen, Geoff Cooke and Dick Best.

I had hoped to be picked as a second-row because I had played almost all my rugby there. But obviously to be a Lion was something seriously special and it made me and my family feel very proud. The squad and management met up in London and the first night I roomed with Rob Andrew. That was something of a culture shock, there was I, an Irishman from Co Kerry with a background in gaelic football and in the other bed was Rob who had gone to college in Cambridge University and so forth. I turned up with my gear bag and he had his brief case and the gear bag. He had all his portfolios and that and I was thinking this fella is very organised. He seemed to be on the 'phone all the time but I suppose that's the way I'd be now, it all comes with experience.

It was fantastic to be going on tour with all these great players. I think I got on alright with most of them, I certainly didn't make any enemies and made quite a few friends. I got on particularly well with the Scottish guys. The tour was kind of funny, like all tours it developed into an A team and B team situation. We won the first four games and at that stage the battle for places was keen. I couldn't really say I got on great with Dick Best who was the forwards coach. Dick Best is Dick Best. You either go with or go against him and I suppose a lot of the guys went against him probably because they didn't understand him.

He's fairly abrasive and very direct and there's no middle line with him. 'Twas his way or no way. It's said he had something about Irish people and he probably had and it's kind of ironic that he wound up coaching London Irish, he had gone the full circle. On that Lions tour, I wouldn't have put my money on him coaching London Irish seven or eight years later, I didn't think he'd be that kind of material, but as it turned out he was and he did a good job for them.

I sensed from the very start it was going to be very hard, everybody wanted to take the scalp of the Lions. I played in the first game against North Auckland at wing-forward and it was great to pull on the famous red jersey and we won well. I also played against Canterbury and now they're hardy boys and we beat them and I scored a try which I was delighted with because I had also played against them for Ireland the previous year and they gave us a bit of a hiding.

Then came the game against Otago and there were a few incidents. I came in for Martin Bayfield towards the end of the match and afterwards Wade Dooley had to go home because his father died and they replaced him with Martin Johnson and that effectively was the beginning of his career. Otago won well and now it was coming up to the first Test. The games were very competitive, nothing easy out there. I was on the team that won against Southland in the match immediately before the first Test, I felt I had a good chance of being at least a sub against the All Blacks for I felt I could cover each of the back five positions. But they picked Mike Teague, which didn't make a lot of sense to me for he was just a back-row player but he was there for his experience and it's something you have to deal with.

We should have won that game but Grant Fox kicked a penalty in the last minute and they beat us by a couple of points. That was a bit of a downer, not good for morale, for it was a game we could have won but let it slip away. The whole squad pulled together - until the next Test side was picked and the three Scottish forwards, Kenny Milne, Paul Burnell and Andy Reed, were all dropped. That more than anything caused a bit of a split in the camp. The Scots were bitterly disappointed and the English were delighted because they now had seven in the pack. Along with our own Nick Poppwell, who had a marvellous game and emerged as one of the games finest loose head props. You had two English selectors, Cooke and Best, although McGeechan as always was his own man. I was sitting pretty in the middle of the whole thing. Anyway, we won the second Test quite comfortably in Wellington, 20 pts to 7, and the pack did well and Rory Underwood scored a great try. The result seemed to justify the team that was chosen.

But the mid-week team started to do badly, losing games we should have won, and now everything was focused on the first team. The week before the third and last Test, we had to go down to Hamilton and take on Waikato and they had a fabulous pack, fellows like Warren Gatland, Brent Anderson and John Mitchell whom we all know well here in Ireland, and would you believe my great Shannon pal of later years, Rhys Ellison, was in the centre. Will Carling was captain and for many of us it was the last game of the tour. They gave us a right hammering, I forgot what the score was and it was a shame to finish the trip like that.

I wasn't enjoying things at this stage but anyway we were back to Auckland for the Test and the good thing was the Irish pubs. They were popping up all over the place and we always seemed to congregate there. Loads of supporters were coming out, not just Irish, and it helped that Vinny Cunningham and Richard Wallace had joined the tour; it was great to see them getting recognition. The pressure was fierce, the Lions playing the All Blacks in Auckland, and no matter how hard you focused on getting the right result, you felt, at least I did anyway, that New Zealand were going to come back. Noel Murphy had said to us the year before, 'beware the wounded All Black', and that stuck in my mind. They had lost on their home turf and that's not an easy thing for them to accept.

All the extra press had come out and they were writing about how this could be a famous occasion in world rugby. I suppose it was like Munster nowadays, you try to put it out of your head, but the pressure does rub off. New Zealand came out and played well in what was the hell of a tough match. We were all up for this match, whether playing or not, and we all got behind the team. The All Blacks deserved to win. But looking at the recent Lions tours in South Africa and Australia from the outside, I felt that those tours were definitely better than ours, that everybody was pulling more for each other and the mid-week team was doing well. The 1993 tour was great and we all did our bit but you felt that we could have done more. It was a fantastic experience playing with players like Dean Richards and I got on well with most of them, even Stuart Barnes, we had our craic, we had our fun and I suppose being Irish probably helped in a way because there was only a few of us there and nobody had anything against us.

The celebrations in my home in Currow before I went on the Lions Tour, Moss Keane, my mother and myself with Brid, Ita - Ann, Patrick - nephews and nieces and a cousin Tony in front.

Mike O'Shea and myself churn out the Rose of Tralee.

Lions v Southland in 1993, I'm in the action.

The Galwey Family.
L-R: Thomas, Margaret, Eileen, Patrick & Mary, Joan & myself, my mother Bridget, Hannah and Frances.

Joan & myself

MARRIAGE - AND ANOTHER WIN OVER ENGLAND!

THE LIONS tour finished in early July 1993. I was home three weeks when I married Joan Corkery from Ballydaly, Millstreet, Co Cork. We met in 1986. Joan came from a GAA background but took to rugby so much that she might know more about the game nowadays than I do myself! Her first rugby match was between Shannon and Highfield when I was injured and on crutches. Joan has enjoyed the scene even though living in Kilkenny and working in the same school Gael Scoil Osraí for the past fifteen years. I had hardly returned from honeymoon when I was straight back into training and travelling to Neath with Shannon. The game was still amateur but there was little time for rest and in the autumn of '93 I played at wing-forward in the Irish team that beat Romania in an unimpressive display at Lansdowne Road. A back injury put me out of rugby for six weeks and my next match was against France in Paris in 1994, again at wing-forward with the great Ken O'Connell making his debut on the other flank. I was still struggling with the back trouble and a lack of match practice and it wasn't a great day for myself or the team. The next game, at home to Wales, was lost when luckless Eric Elwood hit an upright with a late penalty. Then it was on to Twickenham where I was back in the second-row and everything pointing to a hiding from an English side that had beaten the All Blacks in their last match at Twickenham and containing a large number of my Lions colleagues from the previous summer. Indeed, they hadn't lost at the venue in six years.

There was nothing, nothing at all, to suggest we were going to beat England at Twickenham for the first time in twelve years. I remember watching Sky News the night before the game and Geoff Cooke, the English manager who had managed the Lions in New Zealand, was there and pointing out how long it was since they had lost to Ireland at home and how he couldn't see it happening this time either. That kind of thing coupled with the fact that even though he was Irish and born in Dublin, Kyran Bracken was playing for England against us, got us fired up. It was as if he had snubbed Ireland in the minds of our team and he was a targeted man that day. I remember him getting up out of one ruck and he had the shorts and all the rest ripped off him.

On one occasion, Paddy Johns turned him in a tackle, giving me the perfect opportunity to remind him who he was playing against. But he wasn't as innocent as he might have looked. He ducked and the end result was a broken nose for Paddy. To this day, his wife Kirsty blames that incident for Paddy's snoring but it can't be all that bad for they now have four lovely kids!

It was one of those games, we were very physical as we had to be to beat England. Simon Geoghegan got his famous try and I suppose they missed a few penalties and we kicked ours and it was a marvellous feeling. After that, we were thinking, if we'd only beaten Wales, we'd now be going for the Triple Crown at home to Scotland. As it happened, it was one of the worst games ever seen in Lansdowne Road, a 6-all draw, a bad, bad day.

That summer of '94, we set off for Australia. Woody (Keith Wood) came on the scene with David Corkery, Jeremy Davidson, Johnny Bell, and it was a good tour. We won in Perth against Western Australia and in another game against ACT I got a boot on the back of the head and needed seventeen stitches. Michael Bradley was captain and we played the first Test up in Ballymore, the headquarters of Queensland. We came up with this move from the kick-off, I don't know whose idea it was, that we would send the kick-off straight along the ground to their back-row forward Ilie Tabua. He wasn't supposed to have good hands and the notion was that he would knock it on. But the ball bounced straight up into his hands and he took off at pace and ran into Brian Robinson and straight through him. Brian got up about five minutes later.

It was the last time we tried that trick. Although the team played OK, it was a bad day for me as I got a crack on the knee and my ligaments were damaged, I had to go off before half time and that was the end of my tour. Coming after the head injury, it wasn't a great trip for me personally. The likes of Gabriel Fulcher and Jeremy Davidson were coming on the scene while Paddy Johns and Franno (Neil Francis) were still there and I knew the pressure was coming on and I felt a bit of a squeeze. Even though we lost again, the lads played well in the second Test and Claw got a try. Australia was a fabulous country to tour because of the climate, the people, the whole set-up, it was very comfortable, one of the nicest places you could visit. Just a pity I shipped so many injuries.

And so to the 1994'95 season and the beginning of Shannon's great run in the AIB League. I remember we played five games on the trot and won them all. We were playing very well but then I was picked to captain a development team up in Galway against the USA at a time when I was thinking I was one of the senior players. We lost the same day and I was only a sub the following Saturday against the Americans in Dublin. Essentially, I was out of the equation and Johns, Fulcher and Francis were the first three choices. But I did come on as a sub and the Interpros went well and I was picked for the first game of the 1995 Five Nations against England at Lansdowne Road. It was Anthony Foley's first cap and Woody's first appearance at Lansdowne Road and we had the bulk of the team that had beaten England in each of the last two years.

There was great expectation and we were going for the three-in-a-row over England. We felt we had a very good chance of winning again but the factor we overlooked was that when we beat them in 1993 and '94, Dean Richards wasn't playing. He was a very influential player, the fellow who could get in amongst us and take the punishment and give it back. You can talk about fellows being tough and hard but he was really something. He was abrasive and one of the few fellows who could dictate the pace of the game and how it went up front. They gave us a hammering, their tackling was unbelievable and they retained the ball and kept turning us over.

The 1995 AIB League win. What it's like to win with Shannon.

NINE CUPS, FIVE LEAGUES AND COUNTING!

THE ALLIANCE between Shannon RFC and myself which began back in the mid 80's has been one of the happiest between any player and club in the history of the game in this country. I am constantly at pains to underline just how much Shannon meant to me during the international lean years between 1995 and '98. Shannon were there for me when I needed them most and if they ever need me, I would be there for Shannon.

We have seen how my attachment with Shannon began and grew into a successful partnership that has no end. We enjoyed immediate success from the time we came together as we won a Munster Cup medal in my first season in 1986 and a couple more over the next two years. I was a member of the side that travelled to Musgrave Park in 1989 bidding to become the first in modern times to capture the trophy in four successive years. But we were foiled by a last minute penalty goal kicked by Cork Constitution's Kenny Murphy. It was one of the biggest disappointments of my rugby career.

By the end of 2002, I had nine Munster Cup medals to my credit. Sadly, the competition no longer enjoyed the same mesmerising attraction as it had done up to the advent of the professional era in 1996 but at the very least the medals I acquired up to that time were a vivid demonstration of the success enjoyed by the club in the biggest and most prestigious of all the provincial cups.

Equally, Shannon's failure to win the AIB League in its early days was more than a little frustrating. When the 1994/'95 season got under way, our Limerick neighbours Garryowen (2) and Young Munster and Cork Constitution had been crowned champions and I feared Shannon might become "second class citizens" where the biggest club title of them all was concerned. As we shall see, I had little to worry about!

Even though I was a raw young fella coming out of Kerry with very much a gaelic football background, winning that Munster Cup in 1986 meant a lot. Not alone had I been hearing about the mystique of the

Munster Cup for a few years but this was also the centenary year of the competition. The Shannon eight at the time was really good, Tomas Healy, Noel Glynn and Ginger in the front-row and Tony Heffernan and Mick Moylett in the second-row. Moylett I thought was playing great stuff and headed for an Irish cap and was at his best at that time. You had Niallo (Niall O'Donovan) at number eight and he worked so well with Sonny Kiely and John Pearse. The wing-forwards were Ger McMahon and a chap from Drogheda, Robert Irwin.

'Twas ten man rugby basically, Terry (Fitzgerald) was full-back and he was kicking the penalties. It was a fantastic year for Shannon as they also won the Munster Senior League and the Charity Cup and I got a lot of matches. I came into the cup team as a substitute for the semi-final against Bohemians. Shannon beat Garryowen in the final and Frankie O'Flynn sang There is an Isle and I got a great taste for it. There was a lovely homely atmosphere and there was always a great welcome for anybody I brought down with me from Castleisland. It was hospitality in rugby at its best and a side of the game you don't see so much any more.

There's a particular match in '87 that I must refer to. We went up to Lansdowne Road to play Lansdowne ... they had won the cup and league in Leinster. We were crying out even then for the All-Ireland League because although this was only a friendly, a thousand or so people came up to support us. I wasn't too au fait with rugby politics at the time but this was a Dublin-Limerick thing and it was us versus them. They had all the internationals, the same old story if you like. I remember that day I was marking Donal Spring, another Kerryman, and Ger McMahon told me beforehand, I know he'll be talking to you but don't you talk back to him. This was the advice I was getting. We beat Lansdowne that day and I remember there was a big fight after five minutes and that was sorted out and we played rugby after that. It was my first time playing in Lansdowne Road and Lansdowne didn't know what hit them, we must have had a thousand supporters up and down the sideline cheering for us. I played well that day and afterwards people were telling me that one day I'd play here for Ireland and as far as I was concerned that was a cock and a bull story but nice to hear all the same.

In '88 we completed the three-in-a-row by beating Garryowen by four points or something like that in the final and I got my first try in a cup match and it happened to be in the final. At that stage, I felt Shannon were invincible, that we were never going to lose. I hadn't experienced losing with Shannon 'till we were down in Musgrave Park against Cork Con for the four-in-a-row final in '89 and they turned us over. To be fair, they had a very good team, Jerry Holland and Donal Lenihan were in the second-row. But that was a big blow to my confidence. No team had ever won four cups in a row in the modern times and I was shattered. But looking back now, I realise it was just another part of sport and by this stage we have lost bigger and better things but at the time it was the most important thing for me.

We won a few more cups, beating Young Munster in some very tight finals, like the day Jim Galvin scored a try in the corner and John Pearse converted it from the touchline when we should have been dead and gone. That was the kind of luck we had and we certainly had the knack of winning finals. The league came in 1991 and that was the right time for me as I had my sights on the Irish team. In the first campaign, I played at number eight and after two games I had scored three tries. The word was out that the league would be dominated by Lansdowne, Wanderers and Ballymena and there was no mention of the Munster sides.

But it turned out differently and has proved a great competition. It has been very important to Irish rugby. If you look back on it, most of the Munster players of recent times had an AIB League medal or played in a final. The four-in-a-row with Shannon taught me personally and everybody else involved how to win tight matches and how to believe in yourself and cope with pressure. Winning a rugby match is not all about fitness or what you do in the gym or indeed on the pitch but how you think your way through it and how you prepare for it.

All those AIB League matches built us up for the Heineken Cup campaigns and without them I don't believe we could have done so well, not just Munster and Ulster but the other provinces as well in their own way. If the league ceases to be as meaningful as it was, you have to wonder where the players are going to come from.

It's a worry for the future. A few years ago, the worry was that the junior clubs would fade away and it's still a worry. If Castleisland didn't play rugby, I'd never have played rugby; there was a time when the Castleisland club folded and somebody else started it up again and I just happened to be around at the right time when they set up an under 18 team. I'm sure there are a lot of very good players out there who will never play the game if the juniors clubs and the AIB League are allowed to fade away. The AIB League got a lot of players interested in the game, from schools to small clubs. It's seen as a local thing. Everybody in Limerick supports one club or another; you bring that on to a large stage and everybody in Munster will support Munster but only if they're successful, they won't follow us over to France and so on, they won't be there. It's unfortunate to think that Munster would have to go down for the clubs to improve and nobody wants that.

Shannon action

The Shannon Team which beat Young Munster in the Heineken Munster Senior Cup in 1999/2000.

I'm tackling Des Clohessy

Frankie O'Flynn does the honours with "There is an Isle" in Pat Murray's year as Captain.

MY FRIENDS IN SHANNON

NINE MUNSTER Senior Cup medals and five All-Ireland League titles give a fair indication of how much I have enjoyed my rugby in one of the oldest clubs in the land.

I doubt if anybody has better memories of their club or a greater number of friends than I have in Shannon. In every respect, they have been magnificent for me and I am proud to call myself a Shannonman.

I remember my first senior match, it was a friendly above in Athlone and we were leaving from the club pavilion. I had a thing about senior rugby at the time and when I pulled up at Thomond Park in an old crock of a car, it was my mother's, a Vauxhall Chevette, I was just a little ill at ease. At this stage, I hadn't met the senior members of the committee. I arrived anyway and saw this fella cycling in on his bike. He parked it up against the railings and came over and said - Mick Galwey, I suppose - and I said, yeah, and he said - Frankie Flynn, Chairman of Selectors. I had this vision of the Chairman of Selectors arriving in his Mercedes but in fact it was more or less the same as back in Castleisland. Meeting Frankie in those circumstances was a great start for me in Shannon and something I'll never forget. There was no bullshit and that was the kind of fella I met in Shannon.

That's why I wanted to stay with Shannon throughout my career and why I did so. People came to me from other clubs and even a few from across the water and invited me to join them. They were all able to give me a reason to play with them but nobody was ever able to give me a reason to leave Shannon.

I'm there 18 years now and I've made friends for life, when you think back on the great teams and players, it's absolutely fantastic. When I joined you had two sets of brothers, Ginger and Pat McLoughlin and Tomas and Noel Healy, battling it out for the prop positions. Ginger and Tomas were generally first choice but when one or the other couldn't play, then he was replaced by his brother. The scrummaging sessions on the back pitch used to be fierce, scrummaging was all-important at the time. If you did well during the week, you invariably did well at the week-end.

Denis O'Sullivan was coach at the time and a great man to get us going. It was then that I learned you had to put in the hard work during the week, otherwise you wouldn't be right for the week-end. Frankie, Michael Noel Ryan, Briano (Brian O'Brien), Bob McConkey, they used to stand on the scrummaging machine and try to hold it against us. Great memories - but Frankie was the man, the Chairman of Selectors was God for a young Kerryman just arrived on the scene.

He was a man with unbelievable passion. I remember after winning one of the cups, he came up to me and pulled me in and said - Mick Galwey, I love you. We were probably down in Angelas and he was singing all the Shannon songs and the old songs and you could listen to him forever. They all came down to Castleisland after winning the cup in '86 and Frankie sang for everyone and got them all interested. Frankie did more for rugby than I did in Castleisland in the early days. He showed them the great social side of the thing and that they had nothing to fear coming up to Shannon, that there would always be a welcome for them and there was. I did have a good following over the years and still do.

Briano was president the first year I was in Shannon and he came round and did it all again. Michael Noel Ryan, Frank Gallagher and Mick McLoughlin, all great friends and a huge help to me.

Then there was Noel Healy, the Budda, the man who stands out as the real Shannon character. To come back after being out for six or seven years with a serious knee injury was fantastic. He was one of the first I know of to use weights, he was ahead of his time in that respect. He started back with a few sessions on the back pitch, then a game here and there, and proved wrong all those who said he'd never play for Shannon again. On top of that he went on to win twelve or thirteen Munster caps. He played against Australia and that was a success story in itself.

The persistence of the guy was terrific. He'd be dropped but never give up and he was 36 or 37 when he got his first cap for Munster. He loved that. He got his tracksuit and wore it all the time, so much so that people said he'd need an operation to get it removed but it showed how much it meant to him to play for Munster. During the matches, you'd see Noel running up and down the sideline when the others were sitting down on the bench and the crowd would start chanting "Budda, Budda" trying to get him on. One time he replaced me in a match against Instonians and got a great kick out of that. A great guy with a big heart.

How things have changed. When the AIB League began, we'd go up and down by train in the one day and you'd even pay a fiver towards the fare. Later, the plan was - go up on Friday, have dinner in the Shannon pavilion before we left and another on arrival and stay in the best hotel - play the game and the bus is packed with beer or whatever for the return journey. Now it's gone another stage where it's become even more professional and we hardly have a drink after a Heineken Cup Match. We used to but now it's one or two drinks and you immediately start preparing for the following week. Fellas have to watch themselves and be right when it comes to training on Monday morning.

It's difficult to convince people that rugby is a job these days and a tough job as well. Once the season begins, it's a seven-day week. Take the pool work on a Sunday, I find that very good, but it's not something we would have done in the old days. It's now about recovery and being fit for training the following week.

The last eight years have been great for both Shannon and Munster. The Heineken Cup has been fantastic for rugby. It was bigger than the clubs but not as big as International. It gave the players the chance to compete almost at International level. You're coming up against the best players in Europe and those coming up from the Southern Hemisphere under tough conditions and it means a high standard of rugby every week. The Interpros have got better because of professionalism. The game in Ireland has benefited. A lot of Scots are going to France and England but by and large that's not happening here any more. That is good for the game in this country because the IRFU have control over the players and they are not being made to play too much rugby. The players here are getting the right treatment and the right opportunities to play at the top level all the time while able to go back and give something to the clubs as well.

I have a great feeling of self satisfaction about how my career has gone from the mid 1990s. When you're dropped and left out of teams, you start having doubts and wondering if they were really right and maybe you weren't good enough. I can look around now and say that I'm still playing at the top level and able to hold my own with the best of them. Munster rugby has taken on a whole new dimension. O.K., the clubs are going to lose out and they realise that but now the club supporters are supporting Munster as well, people are going to all the matches.

It was great to get back playing with Ireland. One of the reasons I started playing the game was because I wanted to play for my country. I set my heart on that goal. I know we never won any Triple Crowns or Grand Slams but we won some great games. We beat all the other countries at some point. The biggest challenge facing any player in the Northern Hemisphere is to be on a team that beats France in France. You can talk about beating Wales in Cardiff or England at Twickenham but the biggest win has to be to beat France in Paris. To be a part of that in 2000 was incredible and that's a game that will go down in history for some of the players weren't even born when we previously won over there. Beating England in successive years was also special.

Yet Munster getting so close to winning the Heineken Cup finals was the biggest disappointment of my career. The first Irish cap is always a big thing but the Munster campaigns were fantastic. Beating Saracens home and away and Toulouse away, it's hard to top that. Every time you play for Ireland, it's an honour but the way my career went, I always wondered if it was going to be my last match. I never felt secure. I'm not saying my Munster place was there for me but I knew I'd be part of the scene and the last few years were very, very good. It gave me a new confidence. I wanted the players to feel a part of it because I knew how important that was and when a player feels part of the scene, he invariably gives his best. I know how he feels because I've been there.

I derived my greatest personal satisfaction from the wins with Munster. It's amazing to think that you had the most enjoyable seasons of your life and yet the biggest disappointments of your life.

I suppose that's sport and what you have to deal with.

To round off the 2002 season, we had a most enjoyable night under the auspices of Tomas Healy and friends in the Lynch Group South Court Hotel in Limerick.

I take a Texaco award in 1999 from Taoiseach Bertie Ahern, Vincent O'Brien of Texaco is on the left.

1995/96 Champions

All-Ireland League, Munster Senior Cup, Munster Junior Cup winners

Back row: Niall O'Donovan, Kevin McInerney, Dan Gallagher, James Hickey, Pat Kenny, Seamus Tooney, John Deegan, Noel Healy, Niall O'Shea, Donal Costelloe, Kieran Maher, Jim Galvin, Conor McDermott, John Pearse, Brendan Foley. Middle row: Bobby Roche, Gordon Cosgrave, Kevin Keane, Declan Tucker, Melvin McNamara, Brian Rigney, Anthony Foley, Mick Galwey, Alan Quinlan, Colm McMahon, Andy Bracken, James Collins, Brian Keating, Terry O'Sullivan. Front row: Melvin McNamara, Neill Whelan, Soirse Laffan, Gerry O'Loughlin, club secretary; Mick Fitzgibbon, Gavin Russell, Dave Floyd, Harold Browne, captain of the winning junior team; Pat Murray, captain first team; Dave Brockert, club president; Andrew Thompson, Alan McGrath, Alan Oakley, club treasurer; Jason Hayes, Greg Meaney and Brian O'Brien. Seated are Marcus Horan and Paul Meenahan.

THE FOUR-IN-A-ROW

THERE WAS a certain degree of pressure on Shannon to win the AIB League given that all the other division one sides in Munster had already done so. Little did we realise that glory lay just around the corner although the portents were good. A very good under 20 structure that produced players of the calibre of Anthony Foley, James Hickey, John Hayes, Andrew Thompson, Alan Quinlan and a few others was crucial to our unprecedented run of success and we were also fortunate to acquire the services of Brian Rigney, my former Irish team second-row partner.

Niall O'Donovan, a man with five Munster Cup medals, was coaching for the second year and Pat Murray was captain for 1994/'95 and we put in a big effort. We knew we had a good team, Brian Rigney was a big asset and so was Mick Fitzgibbon and there was Mazze (Kieran Maher), a fantastic player who had played for Munster but looking back was one of the few not to play for Ireland but one of the hardest club players around and very important to us. Then there was Jim Galvin, a very underrated player as far as I was concerned, he had great vision, a great head ...the ideal number ten behind a pack because every time you won a ball, you knew Jim Galvin would use it well.

We won the first five games at the beginning of a season that would be known as the ten-in-a-row. After the eighth game we had the league wrapped up and all the talk then was whether we could win all ten and as it happened we did. The hardest game we had was above in Blackrock on a miserable, wet day. They had a very good team with a great back line and were the closest any Dublin team came at the time to winning the league. It was the week before Anthony Foley got his first cap for Ireland but the match was so important that he declined the traditional rest. Both sides had won four matches and were jointly top of the table. That was a big test and we won it with a controversial try by Billy O'Shea.

We played well all year, moving the ball nicely, Andrew Thompson was kicking the penalties, Jim Galvin kept us moving forward and Pat Murray was solid as a rock at full-back. The pressure was on us to win all ten by beating Instonians in the final match at Thomond Park where we were due to be presented with the trophy for the first time. We had a double incentive that day because the World Cup squad had been announced the day before and I wasn't in it so the lads said, let's go out and win this one for Gaillimh. The celebrations of course went on for days and after that we had a great tour of Canada, probably the last of the great club tours.

On to the second year, '95/'96, and we lost a game early on to St Marys and then a week later to Young Munster. After that a late Eddie Halvey try converted by Thompson gave us a single point win 7-6 over Blackrock and by then we knew we had to win every game to have any chance of the league. We did that and it was then out of our hands. Garryowen had lost only once going into their final game, a postponed game against Young Munster at Dooradoyle and needed only a point to clinch the title, but we had a very good points difference and would be champions if Young Munsters won.

The same day, we were down in Cork for a cup match against UCC. A lot of people came down to support us but I know there were a hell of a lot of others up in Dooradoyle cheering for Munsters. It was the talk of Limerick - whether Munsters would throw the game and let Garryowen win the league or would they go out and win the league for Shannon. As it happened, they did the professional thing and went out and won the game. We were trying to concentrate on our cup match and forget about what was happening in Limerick but it wasn't easy and everybody was thinking - any news from Limerick? I remember Joan was on the sideline - I had said to her, if we make eye contact, give me the thumbs up or down depending on how Munsters are doing and I caught sight of her in the second half and she was smiling but I kind of got the message wrong and I thought she had the thumbs down and I was worried.

At the same time, we had a game to win against UCC. As it turned out, we were winning that well ... and then the news came through that Munsters were flying against Garryowen and all of a sudden we backed off the College game and we were hugging one another and giving high fives as they went over for a try. If you had a camera, you would have got an incredible picture.

It was unbelievable - but there was still more work to do because the pressure was now on to become the first team to pull off the cup and league double in the one year. We won the Munster Junior Cup and then met Cork Con in Cork for the grand slam. We had never beaten them in the final in Cork so that was added pressure; we were thirteen points or so behind at half time but got within three or four points with a few minutes to go when I got the ball about five yards from their line and I was about to have a go when I saw Pat Murray coming out of the corner of my eye and I popped the ball to Pat and he ran down the blind side and scored in the Sundays Well corner. It completed a great year for Shannon, we had wiped the board in the big competitions.

A couple of days later the IRFU gave out their first contracts, maybe 25 or 30. Murray Kidd and Pa (Pat Whelan) were in Cork for the final and maybe they liked what they saw and I got one. It was a great time for everybody in Shannon; I remember the day before the cup final, they had the Peace International at Lansdowne Road and we were introduced to the crowd to parade the AIB League trophy around the place and we made the most of it, I think they had to hunt us off the pitch eventually. For some of the lads, it was their first time gracing Lansdowne Road and they were in no hurry coming off.

The three-in-a-row, I have to be honest, I don't remember a whole lot... we lost just one match against St Marys, they got an injury time try to beat us. We had a few very big wins but I missed a couple of league games after being injured in a 17-16 win over Garryowen and I was replaced by Rory Sheriff. They were the only league games I ever missed until 2000 apart from one in 1991 when I took the traditional rest before my first cap. We picked it up again and had the league won well before the final round.

Three-in-a-row was another milestone and a lot of Shannon players were getting on the Munster team. Everything was going great - except that I was still out in the cold where the Irish team was concerned. But Shannon kept me in the picture and this is why club rugby is so important to me. You could have a guy dropped by Munster whose only way back was to impress with his club.

For the four-in-a-row season, there was a new system with the top four teams going into the semi-finals. Lansdowne beat us in the league section and it was our only loss. We beat St Marys well at Thomond Park and then faced them again in the semi-final and it was a different matter and they gave us a very tight match. Garryowen beat Young Munster in the other semi-final and now you had the top two teams in the league facing each other in an all-Limerick final at Lansdowne Road. They said it should have been in Thomond Park but 'twould never have held the crowd.

I'll never forget the warm-up. Whatever way I twisted my arm, I tore the muscle of my right arm off the bone. I had to get a pain killing injection and have it all bandaged up. When the game ended and the pain killers wore off, I was in some pain. But that was another great day, it showed everybody how good Shannon were, we had been top of the league and deserved the title because of that. It was a good occasion and to be presented with the cup at Lansdowne Road and Frankie singing the Isle, it was extra special. Another great day for Limerick rugby.

Playing against England, I was to see a lot of Leicester's "Johnno", Martin Johnston.

Ireland against Wales in 1991

Winning with Shannon and Alan Quinlan in 1995.

On the charge against Wales in 1993, Emyr Lewis and Mike Ford are not far away.

KICKED IN THE TEETH

I DIDN'T realise it at the time but when I was dropped after that 1995 defeat by England, my career was about to take a serious downward trend. Playing well for Munster and especially for Shannon, I found myself being pushed into the international background and I couldn't understand why.

I felt I played ok against England who were simply much too good on that day but I was one of those dropped for the next game against Scotland. Gerry and Noel Murphy remained the management team and Pa Whelan was coaching the forwards and the other selectors were Joey Miles and Frank Sowman. I was still a sub and when Ben Cronin cried off for the next game against France, they decided to move Paddy Johns to number eight. I thought I'd automatically come into the second-row. Instead, they brought Davy Tweed up from the A team and that was a real kick in the teeth. There I was subbing on the senior side but not even good enough to start when a vacancy occurred and that was to say the least desperately disappointing. I should have known something was in the wind but was so happy with my overall form that I didn't see it coming.

Still, I was only fifth choice and for the next game against Wales, Francis and I were picked on the A side and we were beaten that night. At the same time, Shannon had won eight games in a row and the AIL was very big at the time and we went on to win ten out of ten. I was still happy with the way I was playing.

But out of the blue I was left out of the World Cup squad. It came as a terrible shock and was probably the biggest downer of my career. I don't consider myself to be a moaner and have been able to take the good with the bad whether it was in gaelic football or rugby or in everyday life. But this seemed so unjust and I couldn't understand it. I was very annoyed and so, too, were my friends and Shannon clubmates.

The headlines at the time were of nothing but my omission and it seemed like everything I read and everyone I met could talk of little else. The way I look back at it now, however, is something like this. There I was, 28 years of age, and in my prime and fit and rarin' to go, deemed good enough to go on a Lions tour only two years previously, yet Ireland didn't want me. I was gearing myself towards the World Cup, I knew I was ready for it. I felt the experience I picked up with the Lions and the fact that I could play in the second-row and back-row entitled me to a place in a 26-man squad. As it turned out, I was only on stand-by and never got to the World Cup. My clubmates in Shannon and my family felt terribly let down, and while I use the word disappointing to describe what happened with the 1995 World Cup and in the next few years, it really is a cover up for deeper, more heartfelt sentiments.

That was the start of the lean times. I was out of the international scene, at least for the time being. I was on stand-by for South Africa and trained away but the call never came. You don't ever wish harm on anybody but I dearly wanted to be a part of the World Cup and while I didn't exactly wait by the telephone, I did have an ear cocked in case of developments. It was not to be and it hurt and I harboured a deep feeling of resentment.

There was one stroke of luck, however, that enabled me to push my disgust to the back of my mind for a time. The squad was announced on a Friday and Shannon were playing a league game on the Saturday and we won that to make it ten out of ten. That was something good to fall back on, being presented with the trophy for the first time in Thomond Park, it proved a great distraction although in the minds of our supporters, it probably made the sense of grievance all the greater.

I'd lost my Irish place but I had Shannon and the All-Ireland League meant a lot to me. I had a number of cup medals but with Garryowen winning the AIL a couple of times and Cork Con and Young Munster also being crowned champions, we in Shannon were in danger of becoming the poor relations in Munster. That first AIL triumph made up for a lot of the disappointment, I was lucky that Shannon were so good at the time. I would never say I thought of throwing in the towel but at the same time having something to fall back on made it a lot easier. That was the lowest time in my sporting life, the World Cup was one I was banking on and from the outside I didn't see it coming, I couldn't imagine myself being left out of a 26 man squad.

I blamed everybody involved and at the same time I didn't point the finger at anybody and I don't do so now. I never got a reason or an explanation as to why I didn't go. I suppose they didn't have to give me one but there was no concealing how disgusted and angry I felt. I could see why I wasn't on the Irish team although I hate admitting it. But to be a Lion two years previously and there was a 26 man squad being picked and I could play anywhere in the back five, and I wasn't in it ... I asked myself have I gone that bad so quickly. Even to this day, I feel I should have played in the 1995 World Cup. I look at the guys who were there and without disparaging anybody believe I could have done as well as any and better than some.

Disappointments like that, for the wrong reason, probably make you a tougher and harder person and you appreciate it more when you achieve something. I was out to prove myself, I wanted to get back playing for Ireland. At this stage, the Shannon and Munster thing was taking off. I hadn't been dropped by Shannon or Munster, they were something I was always comfortable with and they were fantastic for me at that difficult time.

I would never turn my back on Shannon. I know the way the game is going, people will say the club has to take a secondary role. But I could never be like that. When I needed Shannon most, they were there for me. People like John Leahy of Clareview Motors come to mind. If the day ever comes when Shannon need Mick Galwey, I'll be there for them.

Full-blown professionalism arrived after a meeting of the International Board in Paris in August, 1995, and when it finally came to handing out Irish contracts, I was one of those included in the list. However, my situation in '96, if anything, got even worse. Murray Kidd had taken over as coach from Gerry Murphy, Pat Whelan as manager from Noel Murphy and John Mitchell who had played for Garryowen and for Waikato when they beat the Lions in '93, as forwards coach. Donal Lenihan had replaced Noel Murphy as a selector, it was still the days of the five selectors, and I just didn't figure in their plans, I wasn't even a sub on the A team. This was another major blow - Jaysus, I'm not even in the top sixty. I was still pretty young, 29, at my peak as I saw it, but wondering where to go from there. Then for some reason they picked me as a sub on the A team and at least it was something. Shannon and Munster were still going well and then they picked me as a sub against Western Samoa. This was around November in 1996 and on the morning of the game, Gabriel Fulcher cried off and I was called in.

'Twas a disaster, the first match under lights at Lansdowne Road, Tuigamala beat us almost on his own. In fairness to the Samoans, they played well and caught us on the hop. But we weren't at the races and they gave us an awful hiding that night. Another New Zealander, Mike Brewer, was forwards coach by this stage. Ireland lost two more matches before the 1997 Five Nations, to Australia and Italy, and that was the end of Murray Kidd. Brian Ashton took over as coach but if anything I was worse off than ever. I'm getting rightly shafted at this stage. There's no interest in me at all. The '97 campaign came and went without any involvement on my part.

Then came the news that all but finished me, the document that might well have knocked the stuffing out of me for good. It was the summer of '97 when a number of us got letters to say we didn't have contracts for the following season. I was stunned.

Anyway, that was the international contract gone out the window. Remember that by now this was my livelihood and I had left my job with Ger Wall's Hibernian business equipment firm to pursue a full-time rugby career. I still had loyal friends. Bill Kennedy of Lee Strand, Tralee, telephoned me and said that if things don't work out with the rugby, you'll always have a job with me. I was touched and very grateful. As it transpired, I didn't need to take him up on his very kind offer but I haven't forgotten. Nobody seemed to know what was going on with regard to the provincial contract although as it turned out, they gave a hundred contracts in the campaign to keep the leading players at home but I wasn't to know that at the time the national contract wasn't renewed.

The trouble with Brian Ashton was he believed players in England playing in the English League were better equipped to play for Ireland than the guys at home. I remember when all but one or two of the Irish team were based across-channel or in France. We hated that scene and felt it was desperately unfair. It was a worrying time for Irish rugby. Declan Kidney and Niall O'Donovan started on a one-year contract with Munster and that was the start of great things.

The previous year we had done well in the first Heineken European Cup, beating Swansea at Thomond Park but losing the vital game to Castres because the ref missed a forward pass at a crucial stage of the match. At the end of '97 we lost to Ulster at Ravenhill and Leinster won the Championship with a better points differential. Shannon were going great all the time and even though I was brought along to Irish squad sessions, I didn't seem to be involved.

Then came 1998 and suddenly Brian Ashton was gone in a cloud of controversy. He had been given an unprecedented six year contract by the IRFU but the papers were full of a feud between himself and Pa. I well remember remarks by Ashton such as 'Pat is an Irishman and I'm an Englishman' and after we were beaten by Scotland in Dublin he said something like 'I don't know whose game plan that was, but it most certainly was not mine'. He resigned a fortnight or so later and I think we were all delighted when Warren Gatland took over, even at very short notice.

Warren had been doing a great job with Connacht, we all remember how they went over to Franklins Gardens and beat Northampton in the European Shield and completed the double over both the Saints and Begles-Bordeaux. Having been involved with both Galwegians and Connacht as player and coach, we felt he was better suited to the Irish way of things, certainly better than Ashton who made us all mad at the way he'd go to places like Bristol and Bath, Leicester and Harlequins, but never seemingly to Thomond Park or Dooradoyle, Temple Hill or Clifford Park. Even though Shannon were winning all around them, there was a time when he had never seen them play.

He seemed to look upon the home-based players as second-class citizens. He wanted to play a game that was alien to Ireland, it was certainly alien to me, and he was never any good for me. I won't say he tried to turn a donkey into a race horse in one day but it certainly was a case of changing you from one style of player into a completely different kind of player overnight and that didn't work. Nor do I believe he understood the Irish character and I think even he admitted that later. Then you look at the way Declan Kidney handled thing with Munster, he brought the thing along gradually and for several years now Munster have been playing a very expansive game whereas they had been forward orientated for a hundred years previously.

Then I was picked as a sub against France. I suppose I had played well with Shannon and Munster and Gatland and Philip Danaher, who had been brought in to help with the coaching of the backs, were very much in touch with the way things were going at home, who was playing well and holding their own and that kind of thing. It is said that France were 33 to 1 on for that game and newspapers over there were predicting that they would break the Five Nations points record.

However, Gatland had done his stuff and pulled the whole thing together, even going so far as to invite Irish supporters to fax their messages of goodwill to the team hotel. Over 2, 000 were received and that was good for morale. The lads put on a tremendous performance and Claw and myself came on together with maybe ten or fifteen minutes to go. It was great to be back, the spirit in the team was terrific and the atmosphere was electric. This was a lot more like it. It was the first time Ireland had played at the Stade de France and far from being the whipping boys, we only lost 16-14 and might well have beaten them in the last couple of minutes.

Right: I had the man beside me that I needed in situations like this, no need to name him.

The happy bunch on an enjoyable tour to South Africa in 1998.

Scoring a try

THE LONG ROAD BACK

THE GAME in Paris in 1998 was my 23rd appearance in the Irish jersey. I had long set myself a milestone of 25 Irish caps and now that I was back as a substitute behind Paddy Johns and Malcolm O'Kelly in the second-row, my morale was rising again. Paddy was captain and O'Kelly was playing very well while Jeremy Davidson, one of the stars of the Lions tour to South Africa, was ruled out by a serious injury.

I was perfectly happy with the situation. I was third choice - fourth if Jeremy was fit but I didn't have a problem with that because of his performances in South Africa. Then came the tour to South Africa in 1998 and I was delighted to make that because I had already been to New Zealand and Australia. South Africa was the place I wanted to see, if you like it was helping to make up for the disappointment of missing the 1995 World Cup. It was a good, hard and enjoyable tour with a nice camaraderie. We trained well and it helped to bring the spirit together. Donal Lenihan was now manager instead of Pa who had resigned in controversial circumstances and the tour was undertaken as preparation for the following year's World Cup.

I hurt my back out there and didn't get on the Test side. But around that point I was given a full, two year contract with Ireland and that was great, the security, the guarantee of my wage and I could concentrate on my rugby with no need to be doing anything else. But the injury in South Africa is no help and all of a sudden I'm fourth choice again as the 1998/'99 season gets under way. Jeremy Davidson is back after injury and Paddy Johns and Malcolm O'Kelly are ahead of me in the pecking order.

But O'Kelly hurts his shoulder and I'm back in favour. Munster have won the Interpros and I'm subbing for the Five Nations and that's why I came on against Wales at Wembley. Playing at Wembley was fabulous for me. We went over there for training on the Friday and people were telling me about how they used to play gaelic football matches there and spoke of all the Kerry players who had been there. I had played at Croke Park, Twickenham, the Stade de France, Parc des Princes,

Lansdowne Road, Cardiff Arms Park, Christchurch, Auckland, Ballymore and quite a few more as well. So this was one game I wanted to be part of. It was almost certainly going to be Ireland's first and last rugby match at Wembley and as it turned out I got a run in the last ten minutes or so and I was thrilled with that. Woody got a great try and Ireland won - what more could you ask for!

That was my 24th cap and I was delighted with that as well. Now there was only one to go to the coveted 25th but as luck would have it, I did a pretty bad job on my hamstring and was out for ten weeks. I just wasn't fit enough for Australia and they brought Bob Casey and now I was down the list again but I had no problem with that because I just wasn't right. Unfortunately, I didn't make the 1999 World Cup squad but the progress Munster were making was a major compensation. Woody was back, John Langford came along, Mike Mullins and Jason Holland were there and all of a sudden we had a very good team. We won the Interpros. and played the Irish team below in Cork.

There was a feeling of resentment in Munster that we had such a low representation in the World Cup squad. Everyone of our players that day believed they were good enough. Claw didn't play but Woody came on as a sub, and Mike Mullins and David Corkery were out there against us as well. They were the Munster guys playing against Munster while we had a very determined and useful pack all of whom, with the obvious exception of John Langford, were subsequently capped by Ireland during the season. We had a point to prove, I certainly believed I did, and Ronan O'Gara and Peter Stringer were the guys who later turned the international season around.

That was Jason Holland's first big game for Munster and he did exceptionally well. It was a great day for us. We beat the Irish World Cup squad. Now I know for a fact they were aiming towards the World Cup and mightn't have been up for it like we were but it still meant a lot to us, it pulled us together and gave us a lot of confidence and probably made it easier for the guys who had been overlooked for the World Cup. We had proved to ourselves we were good enough to match and beat these fellows. But the World Cup came and went without me and the Irish performance was very disappointing.

Then followed the England match in Twickenham and by that time I was back in the squad. I had a good chat with Donal Lenihan and he let me know where I stood. He told me I was in the top four of second-rows which I was happy with, that I wasn't going to be picked but that I might be a sub. As luck would have it, there was another injury, this time to Jeremy Davidson. When the team for England was announced Bob Casey and Malcolm O'Kelly were selected and I was on the bench. I came in near the finish and scored a try which is always nice to do at Twickenham. It was also the 25th cap in which I had been placing such importance for a long time. But it was a horrific day for Irish rugby as we took a dreadful pasting.

We came back home and there was a lot of criticism in the papers and in the pubs. A lot of it was harsh but also quite understandable given the pride the Irish people have in the national rugby team. There was a bit of a break and then came the Scottish game. I remember Shannon played Garryowen out in Garryowen in the AIB League on a Sunday and Garryowen beat us and we were all going up to Dublin and we were fairly wrecked. When we got up there Warren told us that no team had been picked and a lot would depend on how we trained over the next few days. So we said to ourselves, this is our chance, all of a sudden everybody felt very humble and that we were all level and the team was going to be picked on who trained well. We had a ferocious training session on the Monday and guys were dropping like flies and basically it was the fellas who kept going who were picked.

John Hayes, Ronan O'Gara, Peter Stringer, Shane Horgan and Simon Easterby were called up for their first caps and eight Munstermen were included and of course to my great delight I was one of them. Munster were going really well in the Heineken Cup, we had beaten Saracens and won in France against Colomiers and generally shown the kind of mental toughness essential if you are to win these kinds of games. It was one of our aims at the start of the season to get more players on the Irish team, it's disappointing playing good rugby for Munster and for Shannon unless you get more guys on the international side. That's the ultimate goal and something everybody should aim for.

I'll never forget that game against Scotland. There I was starting my first

Five Nations Championship game since 1995. I remember Donal Lenihan presenting each of the new fellas with their jerseys and he presented me with one as well even though 'twas going to be my 26th cap. But it had been so long since I got a start and I felt great about it. I felt at least they appreciated what it meant to me, I knew the importance of it but I felt they knew the importance of it as well and it made me feel good. Something like that can do a lot for somebody's confidence.

I felt I was winning my first cap all over again. We went out and Peter Stringer came up to me and Ronan O'Gara was there and it seemed the natural thing to put my arms around them for the anthems. I had seen these fellas come into the Munster scene and I had seen them develop from college players to very good club players to excellent provincial players and now they were getting their big chance. I felt proud that I was playing the day they got their first caps and I knew how well they deserved it. It captured the public imagination but it was an instinctive thing, the natural thing to do, and I knew how special it was for them for they were sure to be nervous.

The same for John Hayes, he was coming up against Tom Smith, and Simon Easterby as well, and they all did great and we beat Scotland for the first time since 1988 and beat them quite decisively as well. John was a converted second-row and I'm delighted to see that he has developed into one of the best props in the game and is a future Lion. Italy came along and although they were our bogey team we gave them a good hammering, we didn't take our foot off the accelerator and suddenly Ireland were playing good, attractive rugby and the buzz was back in the Irish team. For the first time ever going to France, I felt things were going to be right. We were coming off something very good, Munster had beaten Colomiers over there and psychologically that was very good for us to win on French soil. Ulster had won the Heineken Cup the year before and we had all these things going for us and the natural thing to do was to beat them at international level.

We had our usual meeting the night before the game and people spoke up and we felt we had a very good chance of winning. You always want to believe it but this feeling was something special, this was going to be right, everybody was pulling together and the most important thing was the knowledge that nobody would let us down. We were defending for most of the opening stages but we had expected that. We knew we had to match them physically and defend well and as it turned out, it was a fantastic day.

Ronan played his part and then David Humphreys came on and finished it off. At this stage, I was being subbed off in the last ten or fifteen minutes and Paddy Johns came in for me and I had no problem with that. I was told to go in there and do a job and give it my best shot, that's what I was doing. It's all about the squad nowadays anyway and its part of the overall game plan. People asked me if I was disappointed at being taken off and of course I wasn't, it's all part of modern rugby.

When the final whistle came, I was above in the stand with Donal and Warren and we were on the edge of our seats. By that stage, Brian O'Driscoll had run rings around the French and scored three great tries. David Humphreys kicked the winning points. It was just the will to win, the resilience that Ireland showed, if you show a weakness to the French, they will notice it and exploit it but there was no weakness in the Irish mentality that day. So often before we had gone over there and played well for an hour only for them to run riot in the last twenty minutes or so.

The support was fantastic. It was Paddy's week-end and there was a huge crowd. They were down there at one end singing the Fields of Athenry. We all know how loud and vocal the French can be but they were drowned out that day. I think, though, that they enjoyed the game. The one thing I have learned about France is that they are not bad losers. They appreciate good rugby which I suppose is something we didn't have a chance to realise before having so rarely played well against them. When they beat you, they beat you and shove it into you. But this time we had French people clapping us off the field and it was the same when Munster played and beat Toulouse in Bordeaux. I'll never forget the bus leaving the ground that day and the Toulouse fans clapping us and that's something very special and something you can't fully appreciate unless you see it.

Anyway, we had a great night in Paris after beating France. I remember

Woody, Warren Gatland, Donal Lenihan and myself went to a reception in Kitty O'Shea's and of course there was a huge Irish crowd down there. The reception we got was unbelievable, this was before the official dinner and going back to the hotel and getting into the tuxedos. The French dinner can be a bit long, two speeches for each speaker, so they tend to go on all night. Now we were looking forward to it. But Kitty O'Sheas was unbelievable, they clapped us in and the whole place erupted. The four of us had great craic. We did some television stuff and they had the French players in another hotel but it was very quiet over there. What a nice change!

Expectation was huge for the Welsh game to finish the campaign. A million pounds on offer for anybody who scored four, or was it three, tries. And we were there, trying to focus, forget about that kind of stuff, we were telling ourselves how Wales are going to be very hard to beat. On the morning of the game, Lansdowne Road was wet and windy, the kind of stuff we would have loved one time but not now. We were playing a different brand of rugby, we had beaten Scotland, Italy and France by playing running rugby and wanted to keep it that way. Now we were back to a mucky day and we had to adapt. But the Welsh adapted better and it was a disappointment to lose because we were hoping for four wins in a row, something Irish rugby doesn't have too often. Still, three out of five given the start we had was quite satisfactory.

Then we were back into the Heineken Cup with Munster and from there on to America and I got two more caps out there. We tried to put losing the final to Northampton only a few days earlier out of our thoughts but it wasn't possible. Maybe that's not really professional but we're only human, you just can't forget things like that so easily. We should have beaten Argentina but we let them back into the game and they showed more toughness than we did at the end. We flew out of Argentina that night, no time to sit down and lick our wounds, up to New York and on to Manchester near Boston. We played great against the USA and beat them well and from there it was on to Canada where we had another wet, windy day which didn't suit us. There wasn't much left in the tank at that stage of the season and it finished in a draw.

That brought my total of caps to 31. My 21st would have been against England five years previously. I kept going but for much of the time I thought the international scene was over for me, I couldn't see a way back ... well, I won't say I couldn't see a way back, I didn't give up, but at the same time I was wondering would I ever get a chance. Three years ago I would have been happy with 25 caps, now I had 31, and I wanted more. Why not?

In 2000, the first caps for Munster's Peter Stringer and Ronan O'Gara. I felt proud to be playing the day they got their first caps.

Munster's first win in France and we thank our growing band of supporters.

Here I go

A GREAT SEASON UNFOLDS

NOT EVERYBODY remembers the first match of the fateful 1999/2000 Heineken Cup. But I do. It was against Pontypridd at Thomond Park and even though Munster won, we were made to quickly realise that the Heineken Cup was another step-up on the Interprovincial Championship and that seriously difficult challenges lay in wait.

As the season demonstrated, they were a good side, slick in the backs and tough up front, and we were fully extended. Then it was on to Saracens and you could be naming out their big names 'till the cows came home. It was a Sunday game so we went over on the Friday and went to watch Watford play Sunderland in the Premiership at Vicarage Road on the Saturday. Primarily we went to see the ground and get used to it but we also enjoyed a fine game that Sunderland won 3-2. It was funny, really. As we walked by the pitch, there was myself and Alan Quinlan and a few more. Sunderland were warming up and we said to the fella on the touchline, call over Niall Quinn and tell him there's a bunch of Irishmen who want to say hello. It wasn't the done thing but over Niall came and we told him who we were and that we had a match ourselves to-morrow. He was a very nice guy and of course Quinny (Alan Quinlan) was telling him that they were both from Tipperary and got his photo taken with Niall and the arm around him and I met you before and that old stuff.

However, Saracens the following day was always going to be tough. It was a real carnival atmosphere and it was the first time we ever played in this kind of stadium. There was music and entertainment and noise and these young ones dancing around the place and firecrackers going off and bunting and everything. Then there was the little mechanical thing they had for bringing out the place kicker's tee. That was good gas as well. But it was only for them, we had our guy running over to Ronan with a bucket of sand or whatever. No matter how much you tried to ignore it, you were still being distracted. But in fairness Declan Kidney had us well prepared and we knew what to expect.

The start of that game was ferocious. It was unbelievably fast and I suppose they caught us napping early on. They scored a try before we settled at all but as the game went on, we grew in confidence. It was a short pitch, wide but short, and the surface was in fantastic nick. It suited us and we got magnificent tries. Even though we were 21-9 behind at half time, we had come back at them and we were confident. It was the first time we had a really big support away from home and were very aware of it and took heart from it. Killian Keane, Mike Mullins and Anthony Foley scored tries for us, Saracens scored a few themselves, we got ahead and then they went in front again. They were still leading until Jeremy Staunton got a great try and then came Ronan's conversion which I'm sure went over but that's an argument for another day. Later still, there was a scrum near our posts and Thierry Lacroix was lining up for a dropped goal but we blew them off their own ball and got the put-in and then the final whistle went and we could hardly believe we had beaten such a good team.

Incidents like that scrum are what win and lose a match. Everybody played exceptionally well that day, the lads raised their game because they knew they had to. It was then back to Colomiers and this time we were playing them at Toulouse, a ground that didn't have very many happy memories for we had been hockeyed 60 points the last time we played there. Another great crowd followed us over there. The confidence was starting to grow although it was a blow when Peter Clohessy had to cry off before the kick-off. But Marcus Horan came in and did very well and then during the game John Hayes had to go off and Ian Murray came in and basically you were operating with your two second choice props and it worked out very well for us. Woody had a great game and scored a terrific try. It was hard and tough but this time we kept our discipline and beat them well in the end.

Twas funny. The French were very nice, they're always good losers once the game is over, but they were saying you might beat Colomiers but you'd never beat Toulouse ... little did they know. Anyway, Colomiers had to come to Cork a week later and it was an awful day and everybody in Musgrave Park got drowned. Dominic Crotty scored the clinching try and a very good one it was, too, while Woody got a couple. I think we mauled them over the line a couple of times and Woody, being the cute hoor he is, stole the ball twice. Ronan nearly got over for one of them but Woody robbed the ball off him.

The spirit in the team was terrific - we were now a club side really. We had won the Interpros and the four matches in Europe and all the talk was of Munster. You sensed the great support there was for the team. You know the way people would follow their club to the exclusion of all else. Now they were supporting the club AND Munster. The AIB League took over and there were a few distractions. Then I fell awkwardly and got a very nasty cut just below the knee in a game for Shannon against Young Munster and it was touch and go whether I'd be fit for the next Heineken Cup tie against Saracens at Thomond Park. There was a plastic surgeon in Cork who thought I might be out for six weeks but Mick Molloy was confident I'd be OK, that they'd be able to patch me up.

I couldn't do any training in the build-up to the Saracens game but after a run on the Thursday I knew everything would be fine. Phyllis Dolan, physiotherapist, strapped me up for the match, she put bubble wrapping inside the outer strapping, and I never really thought about it any more. The build-up was huge. Saracens coming over was always going to be a big match but after beating them over there by a point and now they were here with all their stars and big names. There was a massive crowd. 'Twas only when I came out for the warm up that I realised the extent of it. Even then the crowd were chanting MUNSTER, MUNSTER and it gave us a great lift. By the time it came to start the game, the place was black. They were hanging out of just about everywhere and you could sense it. The noise was greater than I ever heard it before in Thomond Park. The fact that it was a cold day and people were stuck together and it was raining didn't seem to make any difference. A busload of guys came from Currow, some of them were never at a rugby match before, but they came and had a great day.

Scoring an early try that day gave me great confidence after my knee injury. We made a few mistakes, Ronan missed a penalty and then had a knock on but after he made a great try for Jason Holland, he never looked back. It's all history now how they got their try and a great one it was in the weather and the pitch and all that but it left us six points behind with time almost up. The silence after it was deafening but in fairness, of all the games we played that season, the hardest were those against Saracens. They were mentally tough and well drilled. They played a good brand of rugby. Looking beyond it, even the Stade Francais game and Toulouse and while I know we lost in the final to Northampton, the toughest was against Saracens. It was a privilege to be a part of those games. They were great to play in, absolutely memorable.

Anyway, after that try we tried to put it together behind the posts, let's give it a lash and go down there and get a try. We were awarded a penalty, kicked it to touch, Woody threw it in, Langford caught it, we drove it and Woody got over the line. It all sounds simple to say it but it's a very hard thing to do against such fantastic opposition. Then there was the famous kick by Ronan. It was an awful situation for him to be in after winning it for us in the same circumstances just a few weeks previously. But he did it again and to his eternal credit. There were still a few minutes to go and they had a dropped goal chance again but this time Langford blocked it down.

Then the final whistle and one of the hardest things I had to do was to get from the far side of the pitch to the dressingroom. The crowd just went mad, out of their head. It was Munster, Munster, Munster, nothing else seemed to matter. We were into the quarter-finals with a home draw even though we still had to go over to Pontypridd the following Saturday. We went over there to win but because it didn't matter, we probably didn't put in the same effort and they caught us by two points with a late converted try, a touch of our own medicine if you like.

A clean catch, who said I was too small.

Me and Peter, I'm the one with the hair.

AU REVOIR, AU REVOIR, AU REVOIR!!

MUNSTER WERE now through to the quarter-finals of the Heineken Cup. Euphoria permeated the air but the remarkable attendance at the Saracens game demonstrated that even the recently upgraded and expanded Thomond Park was struggling to meet the demands of all those who wanted to see us in action. To say that we had captured the minds and captivated young and old alike was to tell it as it was. And when the quarter-finals draw threw up a visit from the multi-national, multi-talented Stade Francais, the aristocrats of Paris, the demand for tickets outgrew the supply available. The European Rugby Cup committee and the IRFU had been surprised by the numbers who turned up for the Saracens game and were secretly relieved when the occasion passed without incident or accident.

However, many people who had paid to attend that game didn't see a thing and several beat a hasty retreat to the Bohemian and Shannon pavilions and to nearby watering holes like Hassetts and the Davin Arms to watch the proceedings on television. Aware of these shortcomings, a cap of about 14, 000 was imposed for the visit of Stade Francais and the scramble for tickets was nothing short of amazing with long queues outside the outlets and all sorts of manoeuvring going on in the clubs. The players tried their best to avoid becoming involved as they prepared for the big game on April 15th., 2000.

There was an eleven week break between the Pontypridd game and the visit of Stade Francais. While they continued to play as a unit, we went back to our various clubs and the International Championship took over as well. The European campaign was instrumental in my return to the Irish squad which did further wonders for my morale. Funnily enough, there wasn't that much of a build-up to the Stade Francais game because after the hiding of Twickenham, most of the Munster team were called up by Ireland and there was only a fortnight between the last game of the Six Nations against Wales and the Stade Francais match.

Stade Francais were in the same group as Leinster who had beaten them at home and even though they were full of big names, that gave us a lot of confidence. We had played against Diego Dominguez for Italy and we knew what he was all about. The crowd got behind us on a perfect day and we won the toss and decided to play against a strong wind blowing down towards what they call the Ballynanty end. We knew we would have to carry the ball and we got a dream start. We caught the kick off, Hayes took it on, we ran the ball and before we knew it Dominic Crotty got a try and helped to make another one for Anthony Horgan.

All of a sudden, we were 12-0 up and though they kicked a few penalties, we were still ahead at half time, and said to ourselves, we have the breeze, let's play this game in their half. I know we didn't score any tries in the second half but our discipline was good and Ronan was slapping over the penalties and we beat them easily enough by 27-10. Long before the end, the crowd were singing au revoir, au revoir, and it was an atmosphere I'll never forget.

The Stade Francais captain described them as a cosmopolitan team, full just not of Frenchmen but a few Italians, New Zealanders, South African and even an Englishman, and maybe they weren't as committed to their cause as we were to ours. Declan used to say some of our opponents were playing for their jobs whereas we were playing for a cause and I have no doubt that was true.

Right: Hendo gets a grip

brother
14

A Shannon Group in Angelas

John Hayes, Christy Moore and myself, a solid front row.

GREAT TIMES - GREAT FRIENDS

IN THE space of eight days in October, 2000, I made my 100th appearance in the Munster jersey, led the side to an unprecedented hat-trick of successes in the Interprovincial Championship, started another assault on Europe's best with a fine victory over Newport and celebrated my 34th birthday. In that week also, Kerry won another All-Ireland football title with a re-play victory over Galway. It seemed like everything I touched turned to gold, a point further emphasised another week later when Munster travelled to Castres and beat the local side 32-29 in spite of being fourteen points behind in the first half and six in arrears with five minutes remaining.

Becoming the first player to represent a province 100 times gave me special pleasure. I knew others would do so in years to come, but nobody could take away from me the fact that I was first to break the barrier.

Jeremy Davidson was due to captain Castres against Munster a few days before he gave this quote to Barry Coughlan of The Examiner: "I have played with him and against him and I must say I always prefer playing in the same side rather than against him. Mick is a great captain, a great player and very streetwise who always looks for ways to upset you. He is an absolutely brilliant player who has a great ability to inspire the people around him".

Given the manner in which we battled back from seemingly insurmountable odds to pull off another famous victory over his team, Jeremy subsequently had good reason to ponder those words! I might have been regarded as a player's player, but I wasn't always as popular with Irish selection committees. Gerry Thornley made a telling point when writing in The Irish Times: "Hereabouts, he's a legend in his own playing days, and anyone who'd criticise him or doubt him would want to leave the engine running. Yet he has always had his doubters at national level. It's as if they were always looking for an excuse not to pick him - thirteen times he's been dropped in his 41-times capped Test career".

One of my closest friends is Peter Clohessy, aka The Claw. We have shared many great times together.

We first met after an under 18 match between Castleisland and Young Munster - I was playing number eight and he was wing-forward but - didn't really get to know one another until we both came on the Munster scene in 1987. In those days, you played your Interpro and stayed overnight and had a few pints and that's how you got to know fellas. We were the same age and we clicked as friends and what can I say at this stage ... obviously, we've had great moments on the playing pitch both for Munster and Ireland and a few disappointments, too, most notably I suppose the Heineken Cup finals.

On and off the field, we've had some wonderful times, great fun, travelled to South Africa, Australia, America. We're known as mischief makers and there's a kind of unwritten rule that we look after each other on the field and do the same off the field. We were probably a bit wilder in our younger days and now we're a bit more sensible. There are a lot of things we can't discuss here. We like playing pranks on guys, setting up young fellas coming into the team, checking them out and seeing what they're like. They know that anybody coming into the Munster team has to be able to take a bit of a slag and it's something I experienced myself with the likes of Donal Lenihan and Pako. You'd be nearly afraid to talk at the time but then you came out of yourself and you are all the better for all the fun.

Of course, Peter and I have played against each other a lot as well. I don't think we ever had a clash, although I'd love to put in a tackle on him and he'd like to do the same to me. I remember an incident a few years ago up in Galway when we were leading Connacht comfortably and they brought on a young prop and he was full of running. The first time he got the ball, he came charging at me but I got out of the way and said to Claw - he's yours. Well, he mowed into Peter and I got a great kick out of that. Anyway we're running across the pitch and I'm laughing heartily at what's happened when the Claw trips me. It's one of those trips when you're falling for about twenty yards and of course I hit the ground. So he got even with me. There's always banter going on and Claw's a good man at it.

As a player, I admired him tremendously. You're always happy to go out on the same field as Claw. You know he'll fight his corner and being in the second-row, it's reassuring to have him in front of you in the scrums and lifting you in the line-outs. He'll always give you 100% - a great man to lift a team and you know he'll always do something good in the course of a match. He was very important to Munster and indeed to any team and it showed with the Irish team. I was certainly very happy to have him with Munster and it's also nice to have someone of your own vintage around. When push comes to shove, you know he'll be around.

Times of course weren't always that good for Peter and to be honest I felt there was a vendetta against him. He played the game hard. The one thing about Peter Clohessy - people say he's well able to give it but he's well able to take it as well. You often come across players who dish it out but can't take it back but you could never say that about Peter, whatever he gave he took back and often took terrible punishment. Over in Paris, he was kicked off the field by French teams and nothing was said about it. The Roumat incident was unfortunate but at the end of the day, I think Peter became a better player for it. He proved everybody wrong. He'll be remembered as a very good rugby player rather than for the incidents. There was a time when he was going to give it all up and that would have been a disaster.

In 2001 he was a potential Lion as indeed he was in 1993 when he probably should have gone on the same trip as myself. Then they picked him for South Africa in '97 and brought him back from Australia and his back gave out. Paul Wallace replaced him and went on to play in all three Tests and Peter is now left to wonder whether he would have been the hero coming back were it not for the injury.

It's also nice that our wives and families are very friendly. Joan has been around since I first hit the Munster scene in 1987 and so has Anna and now their kids Luke and Jane and Neasa and Ailbhe are good pals as well. Then there was Philip Danaher and his wife, Eimear, and their little girl Rebecca who Neasa adores. He has stopped playing but we're all still great friends. I first came across him playing gaelic football for a Castleisland district team against Feale Rangers. After that, we played for Munster and then on the tour to France in '88 and on to the Irish side.

Of course we all played for different clubs and I remember the times when they used to be slagging me about the AIB League medals they had with Garryowen and Young Munster while Shannon hadn't won any at the time. That's all changed now and I can throw a few back at them and there was always that bit of fun and banter.

John Fitzgerald, Pako to just about everyone, was also a good mate of mine. He was there the first time I played for Ireland and we used to travel up and down to Dublin for the week-end sessions and he was good old craic. We'd all meet up after our matches here in Limerick and often we'd stop off on the way up and down and you'd have to be wide awake in that company. You'd be coming home on the Sunday and very tired but if you dozed off, you woke up to discover you were on fire or your shoe laces were tied on to the door.

Claw, Philip, Mick Fitzgibbon, Richie Wallace, Pako, myself, they used to call us the Limerick under 14s. Willie Anderson christened us that because we were always laughing and in good form and looking for a bit of fun. But we took our rugby very seriously. When I came into the scene first, I listened to and learned from guys like Donal Lenihan, Willie Anderson and Brian Rigney. There was always keen competition for places. Some of the sessions we'd have up there on Sunday mornings were fierce and that would be after playing a match on the Saturday. Lots of guys with points to prove.

Of the Ulster lads, I became very friendly with Paddy Johns although I can honestly say there wasn't any player I didn't get on with or didn't get on with me. In New Zealand, he knocked around with Mick Fitzgibbon and myself so much that he became known as the third Shannonman. He had to learn the Isle and while I would never say I was a good singer, I'd have to say he wasn't the best at it. Paddy and I used to go for the same place but at the end of the day, we were great buddies.

Something that often amazes me is the massive time span since I first came on the scene. Yeah, I've been very lucky to be able to play for so long. Claw was the same. I've made so many great friends. One was Dessie Fitzgerald. I always felt he wanted to be a culchie, he was more of a countryman than any of the other Dubs.

Life with the Lions was a great thrill. To be able to say you played on the same teams as Dean Richards - and he was a real class act on the field and a good bit of fun once you got to know him - Wade Dooley, all those fellows who won two or three Grand Slams and Triple Crowns. They were grand guys and if I met them to-day I know we'd have a good chat. Stuart Barnes was the guy who introduced me to Mexican food and he always spoke his mind. The Welsh fellas were a bit clannish which is a good thing I suppose. Nick Popplewell was the only other Irishman on the 1993 Lions Tour and indeed he finished up in the Test pack with seven Englishmen. I enjoyed it very much and it was even easier for me when Richie Wallace and Vinny Cunningham came out. The Scottish guys, Gavin Hastings, Scott Hastings, Peter Wright and the others, I got on very well with them. If the Welsh beat you, they'll rub it into you and if they lose they're too upset to talk to you. Either way, the Scots are good craic after the game and they'd be closer to ourselves than anyone else.

In New Zealand, there were Sean Fitzpatrick and Zinzan Brooke. They were fellas you could talk to and they'd remember you. Two fabulous players. I knew a lot of Australians as well. They love winning and don't hide their feelings. David Campese was the guy you'd love to get your hands on but never could and you had to admire him for that. He was arrogant but he was arrogant with everybody. He'd give out about everything. First and foremost, he was a great rugby player while his arrogance was amusing. Marc Cecillon, the French number eight who I think finished up in the second-row, and Philippe Sella, he was an outstanding player and it's not surprising he got more than a hundred caps.

In my native Kerry, during the filming of Fields of Gold.

WHAT THEY THINK OF GAILLIMH

THE YEAR is 2000 and Mick Galwey is a legendary figure as he leads Munster in search of their Holy Grail - the Heineken Cup. Here is what his comrades think of Gaillimh.

KEITH WOOD, Irish team captain:
IT is half time in the Stade de France. Ireland have proved over the opening forty minutes that they can beat the French in Paris. Skipper Keith Wood is determined that the impetus should be maintained. Before he sets about hammering the message home, Woody swigs down a pint and more of water.

Then he starts the message. The tone is right and the others like what they are hearing. But the sudden intake of liquid is taking its toll and as Keith's rallying call reaches its crescendo, it all comes tumbling up and the nausea takes over. So, too, does Mick Galwey.

"At the last line, I threw up", admits Woody. "But Gaillimh just finished it off, he knew exactly what I was going to say. When you have four or five guys thinking along the same lines, you've cracked it".

People like Keith Wood are hard men. He has proved it time and time again on the field of play, he is respected the rugby world over. He is captain of Ireland - but he is not captain of Munster. Mick Galwey is. This might sound like a contradiction but to Woody such a perception couldn't be further from the truth.

"Not so in any way", he insists. "In a Munster context, he would rely heavily on me, in an Irish context I would rely as heavily if not more so on him. He is the archetypal passionate rugby player that everyone can come to terms with, everybody can see what he has and what he has is the ability to say the right thing at the right time".

DECLAN KIDNEY, Munster coach:
Galwey's Munster coach is Declan Kidney, himself a quiet but considerable achiever, and not one given to throwing compliments

where they don't belong. Where his captain is concerned, however, Kidney doesn't hold back.

"He's the kind of guy who comes in and says I'll do my bit, I hope the rest of you will follow me", explained the coach. "His decision making is terrific, what options to go with. I'll take you back to the Dunvant game at the very start of one of the seasons. Time was almost up and we were down three when we got an attacking penalty and Mick decided to go for a scrum and we scored to win the match by two points. I said to him afterwards, that was a great decision, to have the courage to go for the win rather than settle for the draw. He just said - I thought we were down by five.

"In any event, anybody who gets too serious in the Munster squad is fined. No, the respect for Mick has been built up over the years, they know there's no bravado in his talking, if he asks for something it's because they know he's done it himself and that's why they'll go out and do it themselves.
"He's a real team player and that feeds into the team ethic, he'll take a slagging as well as giving it. Mick himself will agree he has a number of leaders around him and you need that. Against Ulster, the first scrum went down and Peter (Clohessy) got a spasm up the side of his leg. Now, the World Cup was only three weeks away and Peter was going and Mick wasn't but this was a game the team badly wanted to win. Obviously Peter was thinking of going off but Mick said, Claw you can't do that to me. Alright so, Peter said, and played on for another 78 minutes. Players won't do that for everybody".

RONAN O'GARA, Munster, Ireland and Lions out-half:
"It's only when he leaves that people will appreciate what he has meant, there will be a big gap to fill", says the number ten. "Mick mightn't be as noticeable to the public, but once he's in the room, the banter between the young and the old is another thing, a lot of the craic will be gone when he retires".

ANTHONY FOLEY, Munster and Ireland number eight:
"We were warming up for the AIB League final in 1998, doing a few line-outs, and I came around the front and hit Mick on the arm and we

discovered afterwards that he had ripped his bicep", says Anthony. "But there was no complaining, he simply went into the physio's room and got strapped up and played the whole match. He didn't whinge or say a word, he's that kind of guy, the team comes before the individual. What more can I say? Well, he's not much of a golfer!

"But out on the pitch, if ever you're in trouble, he'll pull you together. We were over in Colomiers and leading at half time. He explained that this was the first time he'd ever led at half time in a match in France and told us to trust in ourselves, and when we looked at him and saw the emotion he was showing, it just lifted everybody. When we trailed by six points against Saracens at Thomond Park, there was no panic, he just called the penalty kick to touch and it worked. The younger players look up to him as a leader, they follow his example on the pitch - not off it!".

TOM TIERNEY, Munster and Ireland scrum-half:
"If he says something, everyone stops and listens, but it's not just listening for the sake of listening. He's the best man to have the craic but when it's serious, like on the field of play, he leads from the front, if there's anything going wrong, he looks after the younger guys, if there's any hassle, he looks after it. It's an honour to play with him and the other big names. And off the field, you couldn't find a friendlier man.

"A few funny stories? Unfortunately, they'd be unprintable. The carry on himself and Claw got up to, it's as childish as you'll ever find, you'd want to be very wary of the hot spoons going around at tea time. When there's messing to be done, the captain and his lieutenant Clohessy are the main boys but then when there's serious work to be done, they're always the same main boys at the front".

JOHN KELLY, Munster and Ireland winger:
"He's a very good guy, a very nice guy, he's funny, he's witty", says John. "We all look up to him. He's a character, he always has a smile on his face and he's never in a bad mood, the kind of fellow you'd follow anywhere. He always gives 100%, the hardest worker on the pitch, and he's willing to do anything for you and you want to repay

that favour. He puts his heart and sou. into it whether it's a friendly or the Heineken Cup, that's a role model for anybody. He comes around to every player before a match and it only needs two sentences, something good he remembers from the previous match that puts you in the right frame of mind".

BRENDAN O'DOWD, Munster Branch President, 1999/2000:
"His team talk at half time at Watford made a huge difference. Then when we went six points behind at the end of the Saracens game in Thomond Park, he just insisted they would go back down and get a seven pointer and that's what happened, the lads just couldn't let him down. As for the Branch, even during the International season when he might have had other things on his mind, he'd come to me and say, don't worry, we're focused".

Scoring a try in a Thomond Park with grassy banks

John Kelly under pressure against Toulouse

My friends Dennis Kelly and Brendan Walsh in Bordeaux.

VICTORY OVER TOULOUSE!

MUNSTER RUGBY had dined out on the 1978 defeat of the otherwise unbeaten All Blacks at Thomond Park for a very long time - rightly and understandably so. But the present generation of players had only a very sketchy memory of that famous day and even those most closely associated with Graham Mourie's men 22 years previously recognised that Munster rugby was in need of new heroes. A number of the stars of '78, including Tony Ward, Moss Keane, Brendan Foley (father of number 8 Anthony) and Colm Tucker, were in Bordeaux and to a man they accepted that a Munster victory that day, coming on top of all that had already been achieved, would push even their achievement into the shade.

So now we're into the semi-final. We had the christening of John Langford's baby in St Marys Church in Limerick and after that we went out to Anthony Foley's house in Killaloe. We were all waiting now for news of the draw so I decided to ball hop Quinny and told him we were drawn against Toulouse. He replied straight away: I know that. For once, I could see he wasn't kidding. I think nobody wanted to play Munster in Ireland - or Toulouse in the south of France. Oh, Jaysus, I said to him, the joke's on me, are you serious, and he said, yeah, I just heard it on the radio. We were all there for the christening party and the reaction one by one was, oh God, no.

For the first hour or so, I'd have to admit it, I was down a bit but then Claw came in and somebody said Toulouse and he laughed and said, so what, bring them all on, it didn't bother him at all. There was a big break again between matches, something like six weeks, and we were back to the clubs. In fairness to Declan, he gave us all the positives and talked about the time they had beaten us 60 points and that we had only myself, Anthony Foley and Dominic Crotty hanging over from the previous time. On the other hand, they had nine or was it eleven of that side and had brought in guys like Stensness from New Zealand and a few more Internationals and they really were a crack side.

The big consolation was that the match was in Bordeaux and not

Toulouse. Again there was fierce demand for tickets and flights and how people would get down there and there was the story even of the two guys going by motor bike. The whole thing was beyond all expectation. 50% of the people thought we were going to win and 50% wanted us to win but didn't think we could do it, they were kind of sorry for us that we had drawn Toulouse away.

Myself? As the weeks went by and we trained and the whole thing got nearer, I won't say we were confident but we had no fear of them at the same time, we sensed that if we played to our potential and put the whole thing together, that we had a very good chance. Ireland had beaten France and Munster had beaten Colomiers over there and the French monkey was off our back at this stage.

Having won in France with Ireland was massive. There had been five Toulouse players on the French team in Paris and the word was that they were out for revenge, Pelous the captain, the two props Tournaire and Califano, and so on. John Hayes had done very well against Califano and people were wondering was it a once-off. But he had another great game and Claw was very comfortable against Tournaire. They were renowned props, but we didn't give them an inch. Then there were the two blondy fellas in the back-row. They were so strong and fast and almost impossible to knock over.

Above all, there was the heat. Scorching. The end of May in the south of France. We went to the ground, the Stade Lescure, for a look around on the Friday. It was casual stuff, the forwards practising their dropped goals and the backs practising their line-outs, that's the way it was. Totally relaxed. People might have looked at the Munster team at this late stage of such a major competition and thought they weren't professional at all. But they would have been wrong. It was a happy place to be, a fun place to be.

Then the Toulouse team arrived. The people present and the groundsmen clapped them in. The way they walked, the way they carried themselves, yeah they were professional in appearance alright but you could see they were trying to be intimidating as well. They were cocksure of themselves. But we looked at them and felt these are just ordinary fellas like ourselves, what's the problem here? I was glad we met them, especially for the lads who hadn't played international or against Toulouse before, they could see they were all blood and flesh like the rest of us. They were coming in as we were going out and there were a few hellos and bonjours back and forth and that was fine.

I woke up in the middle of the night and 'twas pouring. In the morning it was gone to such an extent that I wondered if I had been dreaming! Declan did a really good job in building us up, reassuring us there wasn't a problem, that we were good enough and that we had beaten good teams, that while we were playing away from home, so, too were they and that worked in our favour. We togged out and came out on to the pitch and I think it was Declan's idea that we should warm up right in front of where most of their supporters were massed. Listen to the crowd, listen to the intimidation, listen to the bands, listen to the booing. Use it as a motivational thing rather than intimidation, take them on up front and don't be put off by them. They were reading out the Munster team and after every name all you heard was boo, boo, boo and when it came to the Toulouse team it was a case of allez, allez, allez. Looking back on it, it was a fantastic moment to be part of and we were getting very psyched up. We did our line-out drills and we couldn't hear the calls such was the noise.

The heat was a big factor but obviously we had plenty of water and ice packs and were putting them on the backs of our necks and generally keeping the temperature down. As we were returning to the dressingroom, we could see the Munster crowd and the whole side of the stadium was a sea of red. By this stage, everybody had a red jersey and afterwards people who had been to Munster football finals in Killarney and hurling finals in Thurles admitted they had never seen anything like it before. After all, this was the south of France and a long way from home, yet it was full of our colours and the atmosphere was unbelievable.

As expected, they came at us in droves in the first few minutes but the defence was good and then John Hayes got his try after a great break by Woody, things like that are what change matches in your favour, and it was in that run that he hurt his calf muscle. We had a bit of luck on the way, a few last ditch tackles, they had a few knock ons. But we were playing the rugby, retaining possession and taking our chances, upsetting them. They targeted our half-backs and kept running at Ronan, they were particularly strong ball carriers. In fairness I think Jim Fleming handled the game well. I suppose I would say that, wouldn't I.

At half time we were behind but we felt there was plenty of gas left in the tank, that we were very much in the game, the prize was a place in the Heineken Cup final and well worth fighting for. Coming out after half time, they looked a bit tired, a bit jaded, and the heat was obviously getting to them too. What happened next was a superhuman effort. Woody was gone for the second half and in normal circumstances a team would fall apart to lose such a man. But Frankie Sheahan came on and had a great game.

The try Ronan O'Gara scored was probably the best try of the whole Heineken Cup. The ball went through I think twelve pairs of hands, the rucking and driving, keeping the ball alive - fantastic. Then we got the intercept try through Jason Holland and kicked a few penalties and then basically just defended our line. There were some great tackles going in and they spilled a few balls, especially Stensness when they had us stretched. At this stage, their crowd was quiet, their bands were quiet. In contrast, the Munster crowd, outnumbered as they were about ten to one, were going mad, lifting the roof with the Fields of Athenry and chanting MUNSTER, MUNSTER, MUNSTER.

I got a whack on the eye late in the game and had to go off thinking it was all over. But they scored a converted try and there were only six points between us. It transpired, however, that there were six minutes of stoppage time to be played. Even though the game finished in their 22, you never know what's going to happen against a team that contains fellas like N'Tamack and so many other fliers and great footballers. So the final whistle was the sweetest music any of us ever heard.

Looking back, their great players didn't make much of an impact. There was N'Tamack up against Anthony Horgan but Anthony had a great game and made a wonderful run for Ronan's try. Jason Holland timed the intercept to perfection, Eddie Halvey was back in the side and playing great but then that applied to every one of the team. That had to be the situation because if the French spotted a weak link, they'd exploit it ruthlessly. There were amazing scenes after the game, at the airport and when we got back into Shannon. One of the nicest touches was a call from the legendary actor and Limerickman Richard Harris. An English journalist came up to me, told me there was a call from Mexico and handed me his mobile phone. It was Harris to say how delighed and proud he was of everybody and, of course, he was a great supporter of the team.

The following day we watched Northampton beat Llanelli and knew they were a good side. Twickenham was to be the venue for the final and all our supporters were wondering how they would get there, flights, ferries and not just Munster but the entire country as well. I know of people who went to Belfast so that they could fly on to London, essentially they would go to any lengths to follow us. We had a night out in Cork for the kids down there like we had done in Limerick before the Toulouse game and everybody was behind us.

Alas, it was not to be. Northampton brought the great adventure to an end at Twickenham but every man, woman and child who followed Munster through that memorable campaign felt enriched by what they saw and the people in whom they placed their trust. In no way was there any feeling of being let down, rather instead there was an uplifting of the spirit and the body which endeared the fans in red to the men in red.

'Till the day they die.

Joan and myself got split up and suddenly I had to go up through the crowd with Neasa - it wasn't planned. I got quite emotional.

BEATEN BY THE SAINTS!

THE SENSE of numbness felt by every Munsterman at Twickenham that wet and windy May afternoon in 2000 was acute - numbingly, bitingly, agonisingly acute. You had to have been reared in the tradition of the red jersey with the three crowns to know exactly how it felt, that single point Heineken Cup final loss to Northampton Saints.

Bruised bodies picked themselves out of bed the following morning. Nothing had changed. Every newspaper praised the Munster team and their supporters but the scoreline told its own story: Northampton 9, Munster 8. While there was never a hint of complacency or misguided confidence in the players, the level of expectation in the squad, the management and above all in the magnificent fans had been high and to lose with the biggest prize of all within touching distance was almost too much to take.

But life goes on. I looked at my little daughter Neasa and smiled, albeit just a little ruefully. The toddler had been in my arms a short few hours previously as I climbed the Twickenham steps to receive my loser's medal. And as the day dragged on and Joan and I read the newspapers and answered all the calls and messages expressing appreciation and gratitude for the fantastic effort made by everybody, it began to dawn that perhaps second best in Europe wasn't so bad after all.

It certainly seemed so when English scribes, of all people, were extolling the virtues of the final. Few ever had much good to say of the Irish, yet Stephen Jones in the Sunday Times conceded: "This was the day when club rugby caught up in terms of passion, crowd involvement and sheer, biting tension with anything the international game has to offer". David Hands in The Times noted: "If the administrators want to package the image of the sport in the new millennium, let them do so around the players and spectators at Twickenham on Saturday". And this from Robert Kitson in The Guardian: "... far more relevant, if rugby knows what is good for it, were the overlapping strands of grace, dignity, humility and honesty that were interwoven into the tapestry".
O.K., so we didn't win, I reasoned, but if these guys saw things in such

a favourable light, it just had to have been good to have played a major part in such a great occasion. We must have done something right. As the days passed, the men in red shrugged off their disappointment and rugby in the year 2000 being the kind of game it is, many of us were off on a tour of the Americas in a matter of days and had other things to think about.

If anybody had seriously suggested the previous October when the tournament began that Munster would contest the final the following May at Twickenham, they would have been led away by the men in white coats. Such a suggestion would have sounded ridiculous but as a wondrous season progressed and a succession of marvellous results were attained against such renowned teams as Saracens, Stade Francais and Toulouse, to mention but three, the impossible dream became very much a reality. Now here I was on the threshold of leading Munster to the holy grail of the Heineken Cup.

Our preparations for the final were first-class. Keith Wood, who had been injured in the semi-final against Toulouse, was fit again and there were no other worries - except for all the talk that Munster were the favourites and that kind of stuff. We tried to steer clear of that. The newspapers were full of the game with each one having its own supplement detailing the lives and times of just about everybody involved. Even though our side was made up of players from different clubs, the Munster tradition burned inside the players and the fans and there was a common bond. The number of good will faxes was unbelievable. They were all very positive but at the same time seemed to convey the notion that the cup was already won. The message was something like - looking forward to seeing the cup back in Limerick or back in Cork or wherever. Still, fair dues to the people who went to the trouble of sending the messages. Everyone was coming over, family, friends, not to mention the guys who went by motorbike to Bordeaux and those who drove all the way to Belfast so they could get a flight to London. People who had never been to rugby games before were going to this one.

We knew they were coming in their tens of thousands to support us, just as they had in Bordeaux three weeks previously, and there was a carnival atmosphere. Even areas such as my native Currow in Co Kerry where rugby isn't exactly an everyday topic of conversation was up for it in a big way and it was the proverbial deserted village for the few days before the match. The fact that I was the captain and one of their own obviously had a lot to do with it but Con Houlihan discovered another close connection with our part of the world - Dominic Crotty's mother was from nearby Castleisland so Kerry had a very direct interest in the outcome!

We travelled over on the Thursday, went to see Twickenham on the Friday, did everything in the same way as we had in all the earlier matches. We sat down the night before, Declan went through his stuff, told us what it meant to be in a Heineken Cup final. Maybe we were too hyped up for it. Inside, we were almost getting emotional at the thought of winning it. It was never over-confidence, complacency didn't come into it, I can vouch for that. There was always the fear of losing, the fear of not playing and leaving it behind us.

The morning of the match and people were very nervous. Some weren't eating, just snatching little drops of water, running around in circles. Then we did our line-out drills and had our team meeting and everything went well in that regard. We got on the bus for Twickenham. The place was electric. There was some crowd there to greet us off the bus. I had been there with Ireland and never seen anything like this. Queues of people, they cheered us and sang us to the dressingroom. When we went out for the warm up, we realised that our supporters were outnumbering them by maybe two or even three to one. It was a wonderful scene and great to be part of it.

Looking back on it, there was nothing we could have changed - except the way we played. We had gone through everything, covered every angle necessary to win this game. Basically, we set out to play to our potential which unfortunately we didn't do on the day. Northampton were all over us early on, they came at us in droves, but we held out well although giving away a few penalties which they kicked. Then Jason Holland dropped a remarkable goal which was against the run of play and then we scored a great try through David Wallace and went in at half time leading 8-6.

Even so, we realised we weren't putting the phases together. It was a bad day, wet and windy. The last time we had played in such miserable conditions was probably against Saracens in Thomond Park many months previously. A greasy ball didn't suit us but having said that, there is no way I'm making excuses for anything that happened. At the start of the second half, we nearly scored a try, we had them under fierce pressure, but they got an intercept and Eddie Halvey to his great credit showed fantastic pace to get back and save the day with a magnificent tackle. But that intercept still was a big moment for Northampton and a bit of a hammer blow for us. And there was another big moment when Paul Grayson put them ahead with his third penalty and as it proved the last score of the game.

Shortly afterwards, we were awarded a penalty inside their 22 close to the right hand touchline. At that stage, we were doing well in the line-outs and it was my decision at the time to go for touch. Every time we're awarded a penalty in a kickable position, I look at Ronan O'Gara and if I feel he's on for kicking it, I'll make the decision. At that stage, it was an option but who's to know. Had we gone for goal and missed it, people would have said we should have gone for the corner. I'm not a hundred per cent sure whether he wanted to go for it or not. At times like that, Anthony Foley or Woody would say to me, go for the kick or the line-out or whatever, and I'd always listen but at the end of the day, the decision was mine. Hindsight is a great thing and maybe we should have gone for goal and certainly it was controversial at the time. It was my decision and I stand over it. It had nothing to do with Ronan wavering or anything like that. It was shortly after the intercept that this second chance presented itself but it was far from a straightforward kick at goal and I felt we could either get a try off the line-out or a penalty nearer the posts or whatever. We won the ball but they held us out and got the scrum and cleared their lines.

And then to my absolute horror, I found myself in the sin bin. It was a shattering blow for me and obviously for the entire team and something that has caused me one or two sleepless nights. O.K., so they didn't score while I was off the field but on the other hand we didn't score either and perhaps that's what cost us the match. I have never looked at the full video of that game - I just can't bring myself to do so - but I saw the incident on television some time later and it didn't change my opinion on what actually happened.

I am absolutely satisfied that their scrum-half Dominic Malone - ironically, he became a Munster player at the beginning of the 2002/'03 season - knocked the ball on in taking the tap penalty. O.K., I was standing near him but I saw him knock it on. It was only then that I moved in on him and he fell. The referee had his back turned and probably thought I knocked the ball out of Dominic's hands. People could say the reason he knocked it on was because I was standing in front of him but at the end of the day, he tapped it to himself and knocked it on. I played it as a knocked on ball and everything was fair play after that. The referee could have given us advantage, instead he turned around and gave me a yellow card. I felt it was very harsh. I don't hate the referee for it or anything like that. He made his decision, a split second decision, and that was it.

As I walked off, I felt my world was falling apart. I felt desperate. Mortified. Letting the team down, letting my family down, letting everybody down. This was what we had worked so hard for and here I was leaving the field for ten minutes when I was most needed. I envisaged them scoring a few tries or a few penalties or whatever while I was off. Now, they didn't do so and that is a consolation, I suppose, but I have wondered since what might have happened had I stayed on the field. My gut feeling is that we would have won the game. It was definitely a turning point. It was bitterly disappointing from my point of view.

I came back on and Ronan shaved the posts with two fine kicks. It was that kind of day. Maybe it just wasn't meant to be and certainly nobody was or is blaming Ronan. Apart from the fact that we probably wouldn't have been there without him, it was a very difficult day for a place kicker and Paul Grayson, who normally is a real dead eye dick, missed a couple for them as well.

As a team, we took it on the chin. When the final whistle went, it was an eerie kind of feeling. Their crowd was obviously delighted, our crowd went silent. We were in the middle of the field. It sank home there and then. People say when you win something, you don't realise it until the following day or even later. But we had lost and we knew straightaway we had lost. It was shattering. Declan pulled us together like the great

man he is and reminded us of what we had achieved and to think of the great season we've had and let's be proud of the fact that we're here and to think of the supporters.
Ah, yes, the supporters. They weren't silent for long; instead, they chanted MUNSTER, MUNSTER, MUNSTER and sang the Fields of Athenry. We went down behind the goal to salute and thank them and then did a whole lap of the pitch. We had gone anti-clockwise, Northampton went clockwise and we met up with them on the halfway line. I shook hands again with guys I knew before like Tim Rodber and Pat Lam. As English teams go, they weren't the worst team to lose to, they were a nice bunch of guys and their supporters in fairness were o.k. as well.

Then I met Joan and Neasa and the famous photograph was taken. At that stage, I was quite emotional and don't mind admitting so. At the same time, you had to be brave but when I met them, there were a few tears. And then Joan and myself got split up and suddenly I had to go up through the crowd with Neasa in my arms to collect the plate and the runners-up medals. It was fine but people thought it was something that was planned but it wasn't, it was just something that turned out that way. Northampton went up and we saw them receiving the cup and I must admit it was hard to take. We had been at a reception the day before and I had this thing about not wanting to touch the cup and in fairness neither did their captain Pat Lam. I suppose we felt it would be bad luck to do so, now I felt I was never going to hold it.

We were numb with disappointment in the dressingroom. Nobody was smiling or looking up. Richard Harris came in with Peter O'Toole. It was his first time seeing us play and so we said, look at the Jonah, but I suppose he broke that eerie feeling. Then we went to the press conference and I think we put up a good show, there must have been a hundred reporters and a lot of cameras. We told it as it was, made no excuses, that we had given it our best shot and it wasn't enough. The press could have given us stick but they didn't. I think they appreciated the fact that we went around the pitch and acknowledged both sets of supporters, they compared us to England who had lost a Calcutta Cup match at Murrayfield and couldn't take it. They felt this is what sport is all about.

We met the families at the reception and to say people were disappointed is an understatement but that was it and we had to live with it. After that it was back to Heathrow where we got a great reception and on to Shannon where again there were thousands waiting to greet us. I spoke to them and said we had let them down but they wouldn't hear of it, we were their heroes and they made us feel good. It was nearly embarrassing at the time but we were the better for it, they made us feel as if we had almost won the bloody thing. There were receptions which we had to go to because they were our supporters when all we wanted was to get to the Limerick Inn where we were staying and lock ourselves in.

Not a single negative thing was said to me then or since or to any of the other players. That's the beauty of it all. Looking back, we attracted 30, 000 people over to Twickenham, lost the game and yet didn't get a single bit of flak - and that was in such contrast to the Irish team when they were in Twickenham a short few weeks previously. It was uplifting and good for everybody. It was a fantastic experience. To play with the quality of the players that were there and to work with Declan and Niallo and Briano, the backroom team of Phyllis Dolan, Nikki Davies, Fergal O'Callaghan, Mark McManus, Len Harty, Mick Griffin, Ian Fleming and so on, they all had a big part to play. It was a privilege to be with them and to work with them - and it was work. But it was very happy work, it was great to say this is our job and it is difficult to think of anybody enjoying their job like we did that year.

Except for losing that final at Twickenham. With the highs come the lows. That was the lowest point of my sporting life but then again you meet people who were injured playing rugby, who are paralysed from the neck down, and you say to yourself, at the end of the day, it's only a game and how lucky we are to be able to do something we love doing. I was up in Armagh and I met a young fella who was paralysed in a tackle and I said to myself, hang on a minute, I've only lost a game but he's going to be in a wheelchair for the rest of his life. That helps to put things in perspective. We're all better people and better friends for it. I can honestly say that I'll meet some of these fellas in thirty or forty years and please God we'll all be still alive and what we'll talk about is the great time we had with Munster.

MUNSTER SQUAD 2001–2002

Back row left to right: Paul Murray (Baggage Master), John Fogarty, Mike Mullins, Jeremy Staunton, Marcus Horan, Mick O'Driscoll, Paul O'Connell, Jim Williams, David Wallace, Des Clohessy, Frankie Sheahan, Kirsty Peacock (Physiotherapist).
Middle row left to right: Niall O'Donovan (Assistant Coach), David Bowles, Rob Henderson, Mike Prendergast, Martin Cahill, James Blaney, John Hayes, John O'Neill, Dominic Crotty, Conor Mahony, Jason Holland, Tom Tierney, Declan Kidney (Coach).
Front row left to right: Mark McManus (Fitness Advisor), Derek Hegarty, John Kelly, Killian Keane, Mick Galwey (Captain), Maurice Keller (President Munster Branch IRFU), Peter Clohessy, Anthony Foley, Anthony Horgan, Alan Quinlan, Fergal O'Callaghan (Fitness Adviser).
Front left to right: Peter Stringer, Ronan O'Gara.

GETTING OVER TWICKENHAM

THE WEEKS, the months passed and the disappointment of Twickenham was superseded and overtaken by other developments. And reflecting on it all having led Munster to a runaway third successive victory in the Interprovincial Championship the following October, I was able to take considerable consolation from the great adventure that was the 1999/2000 Heineken Cup.

Everybody was apprehensive about the whole thing. We were listening to people on the street and reading the newspapers. They were wondering if Munster would ever get back, if we'd ever be the same again, if we'd ever have the same hunger again. We were reminded time and again that we had lost Woody, Eddie Halvey, David Corkery, Ken O'Connell, Brian O'Meara, five Internationals, a big toll by any standards, so such speculation was understandable. It was never going to be easy and none of us ever imagined for a minute that it would be. On the other hand, the positive thing to do was to look at how many International players we got from last year ... Peter Stringer, Ronan O'Gara, John Hayes, David Wallace, Marcus Horan they're all bigger and better players.

So we came together and starting training again. Things went pretty well for us. People mightn't have liked the way we were playing and to be truthful, we were conscious of some shortcomings, but we won all our matches in the Interpros. If somebody said to me at the start of the season that we'd be unbeaten after five provincial games and have the Championship wrapped up with one series to go and stand eleven points ahead of our nearest rivals, then I would have been very happy. It was hard to come back but it was a reflection of the spirit in the squad and of everybody involved that weren't going to allow one game destory what we achieved.

Looking back on it now, I feel we achieved a whole lot. At the time, I couldn't see beyond losing the final. But to-day it's different. I mean, when I'm driving through Kerry or Tipperary, Cork or Limerick, I see young fellows in a Munster jersey and you get great satisfaction out of that. O.K., so they'll also have their GAA and soccer jerseys but it's great to see a young fella in a Munster jersey. I've even seen guys on building sites in Munster jerseys. It's a big breakthrough for rugby, who'd ever have thought the Munster jersey would become a fashion item. But that's the way the game has gone. It gives you a great buzz to think you were part of that.

Munster's magnificent performance in the 1999/2000 Heineken Cup did not happen overnight. It had been flagged for some time, from the launch of European Cup competition back in 1995 when the tournament started even at a time when the English clubs were fighting with just about everybody and didn't seem to know what they wanted. It was a strange period in the game as everybody tried to adjust to the sudden and largely unexpected change to the professional era. It was a stage, too, when many top-class Irish players accepted contracts with the cash-rich English clubs, most notably London Irish and Saracens, and thus left the provinces bereft of their major talent at a critical time in their history. Strangely, however, several of these very same players were allowed to represent their clubs in the English Leagues while turning out for Munster in the Heineken Cup. In this way, internationals like David Corkery, Gabriel Fulcher and Richard Wallace, to name but three, were able to satisfy two masters!

1995/'96 was a good campaign for us. We had supplanted Ulster as Interprovincial champions and we beat Swansea, a team packed with Welsh caps, in the European Cup. At the time, we had a great back-row, David Corkery, Eddie Halvey and Anthony Foley and that was the big difference. I remember Halvey got a last minute converted try in Dublin and we beat Leinster by 47-45 in a fabulous match at Donnybrook.

That was high quality but Europe was a big step-up again from the Interpros, it was nearly of International standard. Beating Swansea in Thomond Park with a late Pat Murray try was great. Pat was captain of Munster back then and was very unluck not to be capped for Ireland. Then we went to Castres in the south of France with high hopes but the experience of that night has lived with every one of us ever since. Kenny Smith was on the wing and he was a kicking machine at the time. Nothing could faze him - or so we thought. But this was the first time I saw the pressure get to him and he admitted it afterwards. The intimidation was awful. There was a full moon that night and their fans just went mad, they wanted our blood. The pitch was ringed by wire and it was the first time any of us experienced such raw intimidation. There can't have been too many Munster supporters, if there were they were probably afraid to cheer for us. I got stitches in the back of my head, over my eye, it was a really dirty match.

They scored seven minutes into stoppage time and beat us and that cost us a place in the semi-finals that year. Castres subsequently went to Swansea and were well beaten which meant each team finished up with two points and Swansea went through because of their better scoring difference. However, Europe had been good, this was what we all wanted to be part of. The AIB League was terrific but this was even bigger, this was the way to go.

The following season, 1996/'97, we had Wasps, Cardiff, Toulouse and Milan in our group. We played three games in one week, Milan, whom we beat in Cork; Cardiff, who beat us well in Cardiff and then Wasps at home in Thomond Park. We regarded this as a big game because we were playing an English side for the first time. We put 49 points on them with some fantastic rugby and it captivated the crowd and they knew it was the way forward. Dallaglio and Tuigamala and the rest were there but we never gave them a chance.

So then we went away to Toulouse and because we had done O.K. against Castres - and Wasps had hammered Toulouse in London - we thought to ourselves, if we win this one, we're into the semi-final of the Heineken Cup. But shure, we got the biggest beating we ever got in our lives. 60 points to 19 ... we went there with great expectations and RTE thought so too because they had the cameras but we got a real eye opener. They came at us in waves and waves, I had played international rugby in France and so had many of the others but we had never experienced anything like this. It was humiliating to say the least. It was a hard lesson but we realised we were a long way off the required standard, 'twas the mother and father of a beating. A lot of guys didn't play again for Munster after that.

1997/'98 was the first year of a full professional Munster squad and of the home and away in the interprovincials. We won the interpros and then had Harlequins, Cardiff and Bourgoin in Europe. The first game was away to Harlequins, the same in which Rhys Ellison made his debut and is best remembered for me clocking Keith Wood. There was a lot of controversy over that. People will say I went out to clock him but of course that wasn't the case - I was trying to tackle him and I got him in the eye instead when I should have blown him back. It wasn't intentional by any means and while there was a lot of slagging, there was never any bad feeling over the incident and it was blown out of all proportion. We lost that game and by the time the return came round, we were out of the competition - we went down to Cardiff in Cork, the only time Munster lost a home European Cup tie, but the 'Quins game still had a bearing on the outcome of the group. A win for Harlequins would have given them a home semi-final but we beat them well. There is a perception in Ireland that Harlequins reflect all that is upper crust and snobbish about English rugby and that coupled with Woody's presence in their side made it another great Thomond Park occasion.

Ulster won the Heineken European Cup in 1998/'99 amidst great excitement and in front of a packed Lansdowne Road by beating Munster's old friends Colomiers in the final. Munster reached the quarter-finals but as they were to discover, playing a French team at Thomond or Musgrave Park and a French team on their home soil were two different things altogether.

Colomiers came at us a hundred miles an hour and if I'm not mistaken scored all their points in the first half. They were playing with the wind and there was a bit of a hill and they had all that and a partisan crowd behind them and we didn't cope all that well. They played the ref, the crowd, it was really intimidating with off the ball incidents going on all the time. I think the ref blew it up earlier than he should have because it was likely to become dangerous and nasty. The crowd ran on to the pitch and there was a bit of jostling. Thankfully, nobody was injured and we came home in one piece but it was one to remember if not to savour. We were very disappointed because we didn't ever look like winning it.

We learned from the occasion, though. We're on to 1999/2000 now and I had a good break because I was recovering from a bad hamstring. John Langford, Mike Mullins, Jason Holland and Keith Wood joined the squad and these were four exceptionally good players. The first I knew of Woody was hearing on the radio that he was coming back to play for Garryowen and would be available for Munster.

I began to look through the side, we had hookers of the calibre of Woody and Frankie Sheahan; props like Peter Clohessy, John Hayes, Marcus Horan and Ian Murray; you had myself, Langford, Mick O'Driscoll and Donnacha O'Callaghan in the second-row, David Corkery, David Wallace, Alan Quinlan, Ken O'Connell, Anthony Foley and Eddie Halvey in the back-row. That was the making of a great pack. Tom Tierney and Brian O'Meara were coming back from the tour of Australia as the country's top two scrum-halves and we also had Peter Stringer in the wings. There was plenty of talent everywhere else as well and the definite feeling was that we could go places.

We had a trip down to Kilkee where we got to know one another all over again and blended the new fellas into the scheme of things. That's where John Langford claimed I ate the head off a mackerel but don't mind that Langford fella, I wasn't even there at the time. Myself and Claw went golfing and more of them went fishing. We had great craic but we were also working hard, orienteering and a lot of running and it was a good place to start our campaign, it pulled everybody together. We beat Dunvant over in Wales and then it was Leinster down in Cork and we beat them with a lot of the Irish squad in their side. We played Ulster on a GAA pitch up in Queens University and beat them and to do so in their own backyard after so long was great.

Then came the World Cup and I wasn't involved and in fairness to Declan, he gave us a week off and John Langford and our respective wives and Neasa went off on a holiday to Majorca. 'Twas a great break and really refreshed us and we came back to Shannon and went on to win the Munster Cup. I was delighted. People said it wasn't that big because it was in the middle of the World Cup but I appreciate the Cup better than anybody because I was around when it was the premier competition in Irish rugby. It was my eighth medal.

k of Ireland

HERE WE GO AGAIN!

AS YOU will have noted, the feeling at the end of the 2000 campaign was that Munster couldn't come back and do it all over again. However, as the weeks passed and the disappointment faded, a new steely resolve re-entered the scene. As we met for early-season training, there was the feeling that if we could do it once, we could do it again and it was then I suppose I really realised what a great bunch of people I had around me.

Having come back from Twickenham, we stayed the night in the Limerick Inn. But the following morning, Joan and I got into the car and drove to Kilkenny. It was really then that the result hit us in earnest. The team was splitting up and that was a wrench in itself. What should have been trips around the province with the cup to friends, to pubs and to clubs, turned into a bit of a wake for some of the lads but not for those of us who had to pick up the pieces and remain focused on the job. Many of us hardly had time to draw breath and we were on our way to the Americas for a three match tour of Argentina, the US and Canada with the Irish squad.

I had a couple of hours in Kilkenny and watched the end of the Ireland-Barbarians game on television before hopping back into the car and heading off for Dublin to join the national squad. I suppose having something to concentrate the mind on stopped the Munster lads from thinking too much about what might have been. We had a going away bash, getting the wives and girl friends together and that kind of thing, and all of this not much more than 24 hours after Twickenham. The lads in the other provinces felt sorry for us and the loss to Northampton was still hard to take at that stage. That may seem a little over the top but that would be to underestimate just how much winning the Heineken Cup had meant to Team Munster.

The following day, we flew to Heathrow and before leaving there, the coach Warren Gatland spoke to the entire squad and told us how we had to put the disappointment behind us and concentrate on a Test match against Argentina in five days time. It was easier said than done although we owed them one because they had beaten Ireland in the 1999 World Cup. In our heads, we wanted to do it but that kind of disappointment doesn't go away too easily as we were to find out out. It was my first time in Argentina and we encountered a lot of poverty even though we were based in Buenos Aires, a superb city in many ways.

It was as if the trip was coming a week too soon. No, it wasn't that I didn't want to be there, rather it didn't seem right to be there. Winning the Heineken Cup had meant so much to so many people and not alone had we failed, but here we were thousands of miles away and for all the fans who had paid so much money and made so many sacrifices knew, we were having a bit of a ball.

However, we were professionals and had to move on. Ireland picked the bulk of the Munster squad again, the players who had brought us through the Six Nations in which we had done reasonably well that season. We started decently enough and it was a game we should have won. But we were never able to put them away and we didn't have the extra bit of drive, I know I certainly didn't, and I know there were others in the same mode as well. It didn't make things any easier when Argentina beat us and from the management point of view, I suppose it was a bit of a disaster. It was a bad way to start any trip.

That was a tough tour. Straight after the official dinner, we were on a bus to the airport and then a flight of eight or nine hours to Boston. That was a bummer, hanging around an airport until you undertake a journey of that length of time at two in the morning. So much for the glamour of a professional rugby player's life! Even when we arrived, we were staying an hour north of Boston in a place called Manchester and that was another bus ride. If that sounds like I'm whinging and complaining just a little too much, well it's as well for people to understand that just as there are many rewards to be enjoyed from playing professional rugby, there are times when it can be a bit of a slog as well.

The management didn't exactly give us the week off but they told myself and Claw to take it easy because we were wrecked by that stage.

They tried out a lot of young fellas against the USA. Marcus Horan was one of those who came on for his first cap and Ireland gave the Americans an awful hammering. They brought back the bulk of the "first" team for Canada but I had to go off before the end because my back had totally seized up. We got off to a bad start and were chasing the match all day. Rog (Ronan O'Gara) came on and kicked a penalty and we drew it but it was a bad result, really. To go on a tour like that and get a draw, a win and a loss in matches we should have won was a disappointment.

Tours at the end of each season are now a regular occurrence and I'm not sure they're for the best. They can be very tough. Every season nowadays is long and hard. There are so many matches and so much training. I know it's all part and parcel of the modern game but I can't help thinking there are too many matches and too much training. By and large, the players don't have any say in this. They're just told the programme of training and matches. I won't say we train too hard but we spend too much time on the training pitch. I'd be a good trainer but my concentration would last for an hour and a half and not too much beyond that. That's my limit. In a match, you're tied up in what you're doing, if training goes on longer than that, it can become boring. In fairness, most coaches now are into 90 minutes mode and Declan was very much into that but it does vary from coach to coach.

On coming home, we were off for three or four weeks and I'm not sure that's enough for the body to recover. The break between each season is getting shorter and the seasons are getting longer. It's fine for the younger lads. When I was young, I went straight from the gaelic pitch to the rugby pitch and was happy to go for twelve months of the year. It didn't bother me, in fact I liked it. In those days, there was always a thrill, a feeling of excitment, in pulling on the jersey, whether it was that of Currow or Castleisland, Shannon or Munster. As the years went by, though, the need for rest became more and more apparent and it's not just rugby players who see things like that. Even those in non physical impact sports like golf take breathers at regular intervals because mentally it can become very draining.

And then it was time for Munster to deliver once more. We had a pre-season trip to Glasgow and the hangover was still there from the Twickenham match even though we had now moved on the best part of three months. I was captain again and I called all the lads together before we went out and told them that Twickenham was now history, this is our first time out since then and it's a new season and all that. We started disastrously, 7-0 down after only a few minutes, but we turned the game around and put 50 or 60 points on them. It was the best way to put the whole thing behind us, our first chance to get a very annoying monkey off our back. It was only a pre-season friendly but it showed us we could still play and that we were able to carry on. We had a lot of chats between ourselves. Declan and Niallo were very aware of the situation. That Glasgow game was great for us, if you like the mood was set that night.

Crash landing

Quinny's version of the "Nutcracker"

The 'Great Foley', steeped in rugby, never gives less than 110 percent

THE ROAD TO LILLE

BEFORE WE knew it, we were back into the Interpros and the Heineken Cup. We again went through the Interpros unbeaten. The previous year, we had beaten Ulster at the football pitch in the university grounds in Belfast but this time we went up and beat them at Ravenhill, the first time this Munster team had done so, and that was another source of inspiration.

We had Bath, Castres, and Newport in our Heineken Cup group. The first match was against Newport in Thomond Park and I'll never forget it because on the same day Kerry played Galway in the All-Ireland final in Croke Park. It was a re-play of a game I had attended two weeks previously like any other good Kerryman. Kerry got off to a great start, led by seven points or so, but Galway clawed them back and got a draw. It was decided that night to play the match on the following Saturday week, the same day as the Munster match, and I could have done without that!

It was never a problem to concentrate on our match against Newport but I still wanted to know how Kerry were getting on. I'm usually very slow to tog off after a game, 99% of the time I'd be last out of the dressingroom, especially with being captain and doing the usual meda interviews and so on. We won the game, it was typical early season stuff and an average performance but we won and that's what mattered. I got into the Shannon pavilion for the end of the football and saw Kerry win and that made for a nice double.

From there we moved on to familiar territory. Claw and myself had played against Castres down in the south of France a few years previously and we were well aware of what an intimidating, almost frightenting, place it could be. The last thing we needed was a bad start but that's exactly what we got. They kicked off, we knocked on, they won the scrum and scored a great try. We hadn't even touched the ball and we were seven points behind. They scored again and Quinny got a yellow card and things looked pretty desperate. But we kicked a penalty or two before half time to get us back into the game. We went on to play some great rugby in the second half as we have so often done, it was a hallmark of the side, especially playing away from home where we let teams come at us before we got back at them. I know, I know, it was a dangerous tendency on our parts but that seemed to be the nature of the team.

That was a marvellous match, I think it finished up 32-29 in our favour. Ronan got a great try and it was tit-for-tat with the kicks and we held out well at the end. It was great to score a big win like that away from home, it really got us back into the Heineken Cup. It proved again that the spirit was right, it was our first big test, we had come through with a Grade A and naturally self belief and confidence in the camp soared sky high.

The following week, things got even better. We had Bath, one of the great clubs of the British scene for many years, at home and this was another game in which we would prove if we were really as good as our results of the previous year had suggested. Thankfully, that day went really well for us. We gave them a right hammering in front of a packed Thomond Park scoring four or five tries. It was one thing for us to do our stuff, it was another to get the fans behind us again but we needn't have feared on that count. The buzz was back and to see off such a talented team as Bath in such convincing fashion really put the wheels back on the wagon. Suddenly, Twickenham, Northampton and single point defeats seemed a long time ago!

The one grey area was that I took a bad knock on the shoulder that day and my knee went as well but I carried on. The Irish squad was picked after the Bath match and I was one of only three second-rows, Mal O'Kelly and Jeremy Davidson being the others. However, a week later we took on Bath at the Recreation Ground in the return game. The weather was awful and the match should never have been played. It was the day our doctor, Micky Griffin, tried to jump over me as I lay on the ground injured but he clipped my toe and came down on top of me instead. As if I didn't have enough troubles of my own. That's something Micky will never be allowed to forget! It wasn't his fault, of course, but I had knee ligament trouble and I had to come off and I was out for three or four weeks. Kirsty Peacock had joined the physio team and played a big part in getting me right again.

We were well beaten by Bath but at the same time they only beat us on penalties and David Wallace scored the only try and a beauty it was, too. We played Bath in two matches and we got six tries against them and they got none and as it turned out in the end, that's why we qualified for the knock-out stages. I missed the two Ireland matches against South Africa and Japan and that's when Gary Longwell came in for his first cap.

Around that time as well, Shannon went on a tour to Marbella in Spain, just the kind of break I needed at the time. They had been playing in the early rounds of the Munster Cup up to then but the final against Young Munster was fixed for the Sunday, the day after we were due home. So it was a beneficial week from a rugby perspective, good fun but serious for all that. I was able to do some training out there and I was delighted the injuries had cleared up. I was on the bench and came in as a sub for my ninth cup medal and that was very big for me. Young Colm Tucker got the call as well during the game which meant I had won a cup medal with a father and son of the same name. When that kind of thing happens, you know you're pushing on for sure but it still gave me a lot of satisfaction.

With the injury setbacks behind, it was time to concentrate once again on the Heineken Cup. Coming up to Christmas, we defeated Castres on a very wet, windy day at Musgrave Park, meaning we were in pole position going into the break. But it was still a stop-start situation as far as Munster's preparations were concerned and although they never complained, it must have been a pain in the neck for Declan, Niallo and the coaching staff in general. We had a friendly against Leinster in Cork before travelling over for the return match against Newport in Rodney Parade. We lost to Leinster but the game was of great benefit to us. Newport had beaten Cardiff in their annual St Stephens Day (Boxing Day over there, of course) encounter and were really up for our visit.

It was a big ask for us. We knew they were a crack side. The great South African number eight Gary Teichman was captain and again we found ourselves something like fourteen points behind after only twenty minutes or so. Matt Mostyn, who had played for Connacht and Ireland, got one of their tries. Again, though, we kicked a few penalties and showed a lot of character to get back into it. Rog had a great game and got the full complement, try, drop goal, penalties and conversion. We did well in the forwards, Stringer had a massive match, Anthony Horgan got an intercept try that put them away and the best score of all was probably Mike Mullins's try. He was coming back after injury and was a bit iffy fitness-wise but he split their defence and got probably his best ever try for Munster.

That was a great occasion for we had a massive crowd over there with us. They were belting out "who let the dogs out" over the tannoy but our supporters outcheered them and changed the words to "who let the Claw out". Fantastic, just fantastic. The atmosphere was probably as good as anything I have ever experienced. It was also our first time winning in Wales. We had drawn with Neath; Pontypridd and Cardiff beat us over there so this was another monkey off our backs.

It was a real carnival atmosphere. It was a lovely ground, a little bit like Thomond Park with the crowd really close and all around us. The Munster fans came on to the pitch afterwards and cheered us off. They were terrific and there was never an inkling of trouble. Quite the contrary and the Newport Chairman subsequently wrote to us and complimented our supporters on making it the great occasion it undoubtedly was. That was nice to see even though it was a professional game and they were obviously disappointed. They even went so far as to put banners up on the walls proclaiming that "Munster will always be welcome in Newport". It just goes to show the crowds who follow us really enjoyed themselves and it also goes to show that when the Welsh and the Irish get together, they will always have a good time.

So that got us into the quarter-final and we drew Biarritz, who had beaten Leinster pretty comprehensively. At the same time, the word got out from Leinster that Biarritz weren't a great side and that we were going to hammer them. To be honest, that kind of stuff didn't help us and it was something we could have done without. Instead, Biarritz were a right good side and had a lot of good individuals - Gonzalez, who played hooker for France; Roumat, Claw's pal; their open side had played for France; Betsen, the other flanker, was yet to play for France and he had a powerful game and we have since seen how good a player he is; Bernat-Salle was on the wing and then there was out-half Frano Botica, the former All Black and Rugby League player who could kick goals from anywhere. They had a right good team and they started very well against us in front of another full house at Thomond Park. A familiar pattern emerged once again. We started very slowly and they got a couple of tries early on.

Falling behind at Thomond Park doesn't happen to us very often but we came back well and Anthony Foley got three tries and with them, believe it or not, free pizzas for life! The deal was with Brian McGoey, a former Shannon scrum-half, that the first player to score three tries for Munster in the Heineken Cup, would get free pizzas for life, as many as he could get into himself, from Domino's Pizzeria. Obviously I hadn't heard about this, otherwise Anthony mightn't have got the ball so easily and as often as he did! Maybe it was just as well or we wouldn't have won any matches.

Jokes aside, it was a tough match, a cracking match, and Biarritz were in it right to the end. I made a comment afterwards that it was as tough a match as I ever played at Thomond Park and I wasn't exaggerating. We didn't by any means control the game, we were playing catch up a lot of the time and were holding on by the skin of our teeth at the end. Now we were back into the semi-finals again and naturally we were very proud of that given the disappointment of the previous season. If you like, we had taken on the best that England, Wales and France could throw at us and beaten them all. Talk of a flash in the pan the previous season was no longer to be heard, not even from those parts of England where Irish rugby seems to do nothing right.

But then there was a big shutdown for the Heineken Cup and a week later we were off to Italy for the start of the Six Nations Championship.

The Irish Squad in Rome. I couldn't help thinking that those nearest to the Pope were fellas who hadn't darkened the door of a church for years.

ITALY AND THE SIX NATIONS

A BUS picked us up in Thomond Park after the Biarritz game and we were taken up to Dublin to join the rest of the squad. I hadn't played against Italy in Italy before and it was great to go to Rome and see the Eternal City and meet the Pope and so on. It was a nice experience but I couldn't help thinking that those nearest to him in the photo were fellas who hadn't darkened the door of a church for years! But we had a difficult match to win and even though we did so, Italy proved stubborn opposition and didn't give up without a fight, literally on the occasion that their scrum-half Troncon flattened Peter Stringer with a haymaker. At that point, Foley and myself had come off and we were sitting on the bench and Stringer came off and we were laughing at him because it was the first time we saw him getting a proper clatter. I suppose we felt sorry for him as well but he carried on and he was alright.

There we were, sitting on the bench during a Six Nations International, when these two guys from Castleisland (one of them was John Breen) just meandered out and sat down beside me. They decided to have the best seat in the ground and not a bother on them. Dessie Barry from the Examiner was there and got the photo and I have it at home. Where else would you find it or who else would have the neck to do it. That's the kind of atmosphere there was that day, it wasn't like your Lansdowne Road or Twickenham, more laid back and it was nice, a good set-up in a good stadium. It was also the day that Hendo (Rob Henderson) got his hat-trick of tries - and there were no free pizzas this time even though we were playing in the home of pizzas! We struggled in the first half when the video ref gave them a try but we won well enough in the end.

The next week was the French game at Lansdowne Road. This was supposed to be the payback for Paris the previous year but we played well again and this time beat them at home with the help of the famous Brian O'Driscoll try. It isn't often you beat them twice in a row. Naturally, it was a bigger deal beating them over in the Stade de France but we hadn't beaten them in Dublin since 1983. We sat down before that match and Warren Gatland threw me the marker pen and told me to write down why we were going to beat France. He took me completely unawares but I went up and wrote down one word - TALENT. I knew there was genuine talent in that team and there wasn't a reason why we shouldn't have beaten them. There was a great team there. It had matured a lot. We were disappointed at how we played against Italy and so wanted a big performance against France. We mightn't have beaten them by much in the end but we were very pleased at the way we performed.

Wales were next on the agenda but by this stage foot and mouth had become an issue and the word was out that the match could be in doubt. We trained up in Greystones on the Tuesday in flogging rain and the next day in snow. We were watching the news and hearing about all the outbreaks but we carried on as though the game was going ahead. We went down to an indoor place near Bray and from the bus to the hall was 300 yards or so but the craic we had throwing snowballs at each other, you'd think it was an under twelves team coming. There was so much snow and there was nobody around and we were running down through it all, it just went to show we were all human.

We still had the game in our minds but on the way back in the bus, we heard the Minister for Agriculture Joe Walsh on the news talking about all the outbreaks of the foot and mouth in England and Wales and he finished off by appealing to the IRFU to call off the game and not to go to Wales. When we heard that, we knew our chance of playing in the Millennium Stadium was gone for a while. At 6 o'clock that evening, Philip Browne the IRFU Secretary, rang to say the game was off. There was going to be no rugby, no training for several weeks and we just had to disperse. Before we did so, though, we went into Dublin and had a right party, it was like an end of season bash. For the next six weeks, we trained away on our own, we weren't even allowed to come together. In fairness, at the end of the day, it was only a game even though it was our livelihood. But it was not as important as the farmer's livelihood or the agricultural industry. It was a big sacrifice to make but it was worth it, we helped to keep foot and mouth out of Ireland. Still, I couldn't help wondering if I had lost my chance of ever playing in the Millennium Stadium, little realising what the immediate future held in store!

No matter how often I say it, there's nothing like winning.

IT WAS A FAIR TRY. When Johnno says something happened, it happened. I said to the ref "what about the 'Video Ref'" and he replied that they didn't have it.

LANDERED!

THE SIX Nations matches were deferred into the next season so it was basically a bit of club rugby and the recommencement of the Heineken Cup. Even though we didn't have any matches, David Wallace and Alan Quinlan were both injured and our next competitive outing was against Ireland at Thomond Park. We beat Ireland that day or rather a combination of Leinster and Ulster because the English based guys were tied up in their own domestic affairs.

The Lions selectors were present, Graham Henry, Andy Robinson, Donal Lenihan and it was a good work-out for us. They led early on but we came back well and learned a lot about ourselves in the build-up to another lousy draw against Stade Francais in Lille. I remember the draw being made in the Sugar Club, a night club off Leeson Street, and bloody hell, we came out last and it meant Stade Francais away. Their out-half Diego Dominguez was there and the one word he used was revenge, all he could say was revenge, and it's a strong word to use. He remembered how we had beaten them the previous year in the quarter-final and obviously he was still finding it a little painful.

We went over to Lille thinking we were well prepared but the fact that we were out of rugby for six weeks caught up with us. We simply weren't ready and the circumstances surrounding the game were no help. It was far from the ideal place to play a rugby match, certainly not one of this importance. The draw had been bad, now the venue was worse, 'twas a hard place to get to. On top of that, the weather was bad and we had a few injuries as well. I suppose these things always come into play when you lose games. Stade got a handy try in the first half and we were chasing the game for a long time.

Then came John O'Neill's infamous disallowed try. Whenever that match is recalled, it's the one incident that is always brought up and with bloody good reason, too. After it happened, I said to the ref, Chris White, what about the video ref and he replied that they didn't have it. I was dumbstruck. Here we were, playing in the semi-final of the Heineken Cup with a huge amount at stake, not least money, although to us winning the competition was what it was all about, and they didn't have this vital piece of equipment. We felt let down by the organisers of the Heineken Cup on several occasions before and after that day but I suppose in the final analysis their failure to provide the video facility was the worst of all. It cost us the match and it didn't help that everybody in the press box, both Irish and French, as well as British journalists, saw the incident time and time again and were all of one voice.

IT WAS A FAIR TRY.

The touch judged Stevie Lander (or Stevie Wonder as we called him), disallowed the try straight away. There was a time when the Welsh and especially the comedian Max Boyce lampooned John West as "the blind Irish referee". The jibe was recalled by those people with memories of that era but blind or not, those English officials did us a lot of harm even if they were man enough to subsequently admit that they got it wrong.

OK, we didn't deserve to win it on the day regardless of the disallowed try or whether or not a penalty by Rog went between the sticks as again television said it did and the majority of the crowd thought so as well. But there are often games you don't deserve to lose and you do and there are games you deserve to win and you don't. In fairness, they were a better team than us on the day, in the forwards anyway, although maybe I'm being too harsh on us. We didn't play fluent rugby that day and didn't do ourselves justice, that's the best way of putting it, and yet we could have won.

Johnno's try will hang around our necks like a millstone for as long as we live. I was coming along behind him and didn't see it exactly but he is adamant it was a fair score. When Johnno says something happened, it happened, and anyway the photographic and television evidence are all there. He had a fantastic game the same day. I was thinking about it afterwards and came to the conclusion that I had never seen any player so influential in a Munster jersey, and especially being a back. You'll often see an outstanding forward but for a wing, out there on his own, to make such an impression was brilliant. He gave them all kinds of trouble, they were sending in two and three fellas to tackle him. In some ways he kept us in the game. He was our main target man and I was delighted for him. He hadn't been on the team but he took his chance and did exceptionally well that day.

But it was only afterwards when I saw the photograph - and it's a famous one now - that I realised we had been hard done by. On the field, we didn't realise how close it was or how important it was. But when one of the photographers pulled me aside and showed me the shots and I realised just how fair a try it was, it only made things worse. You'd nearly prefer if the officials had been right, it mightn't have made it so hard to take. It was bad enough to be beaten, but to be beaten in those circumstances was desperate, a real downer.

And then we began to wonder ... is this the end of another era? Will we ever get to a Heineken Cup final again? We came together and went around the pitch and saluted the crowd and they were fantastic for they had travelled in their thousands once again. We felt awful as much for them as for ourselves.

Making things even more poignant, Joan was pregnant at the time and she had made a great effort to attend the match. She had to go to the doctor to see if it was alright for her to go to France. There she stood on her own ... 'twas raining, ... 'twas cold and I saw her there, pregnant ... miserable ... disappointed as we all were. It was all very hard to take.

Introducing the players to President Mary McAleese.

CAPTAIN OF IRELAND

NEVERTHELESS, WHEN the rugby season is as long as it is these days, there's always something around the corner to capture your attention and in this case, there was the upcoming Ireland game against Romania in Bucharest. None of the guys going on the Lions tour of Australia were available including Mal O'Kelly. Woody was obviously gone and he was captain of the Irish side. So it was an opportunity for a lot of fellas to get caps; for me it was an opportunity to captain the team and realise an ambition of many years standing.

So I was over the moon when I got the call for it was something I had never done outside of A matches. I came close enough to it in the French match a few months previously when Woody was only declared fit on the morning of the game. He couldn't throw line-outs on the previous day because his back was in bits and I was told I'd be captain if he didn't make it. I didn't want to wish Woody any bad luck but I was getting hyped up about it. It wasn't to be and maybe it was for the best because we beat France, something that doesn't occur all that often.

Now I had the job, even if it was only over in Romania. There weren't a whole lot of Irish people at the match; come to think of it, there weren't too many Romanians there either! It's a poor country. It was like going back in time but very sad to see the poverty. We drove around Bucharest in taxis at night time to see the place which is something I really like to do when I go to a new city. There was a soccer match the same week-end, Romania against Hungary. For some reason, the rugby match was fixed for the national stadium and the soccer match was in the ground used by the Steau Bucharest club. Apparently the Sports Minister was a big rugby fan and accordingly decreed that the rugby match should be in the national stadium.

All the noise around town was about the soccer team but we were brought to this massive old stadium with an athletics track around it so that the dressingrooms were 200 yards away from the pitch. It was a bit unreal. I won't say it was hard to get yourself up for it but it was definitely different. It wasn't your ordinary International, not even like the previous year when we were in Argentina, America and Canada when there was a fair bit of hype around. There wasn't much where this game was concerned. The Lions had taken over.

It was a massive stadium and the atmosphere was lacking. I remember the band gave a rendition of Ireland's Call that was about three notes too high. We were looking at each other and trying to sing along to it but it wasn't possible! Even though we shouldn't have, we were smiling more than a little bit, hopefully to ourselves. It was Shane Byrne's first cap and he was more excited even than I was because it meant everything to him and he had waited a long time whereas for a lot of the others it was just another end of season affair.

Romania came at us early on even though they were missing a few guys still playing in France at the time. Eventually, we put fifty points on them and I scored a try which is always nice to do when you're captaining your country. Mick O'Driscoll replaced me towards the end to gain his first cap. He and I share the same birthday, October 8th, but there are 12 years between us. When you look back on it, what more can you do? It was funny that day, I was about to go out on the pitch and Warren Gatland said "best of luck, this might be your last one" and I was kinda thinking, coming from you, are you trying to tell me something. 'Twas a strange thing to say at the time and I wondered if he was trying to get me worked up or simply saying, you're going to captain Ireland, well done.

Afterwards, we went to this fabulous hotel for dinner. You see the poverty on the streets and then you go to this massive five star hotel, really plush and loads of money, the best of food and drink and the best of everything, all laid on by the Romanian Rugby Federation. That was difficult to take in many ways but from a rugby perspective, it was nice to have played in Romania and other places like the Americas where I got the opportunity to play over the last few years of my career and where you wouldn't normally have that chance.

My second little girl, Ailbhe, had been born just before the Heineken Cup final. She arrived on May 18th and just as well, too, with the big game the following Saturday and all the hassle a "clash" might have created. I might have missed out on the birth of my child so if you like, that was the perfect consolation prize! The important thing was that she was healthy and everything was grand even though she was only a week old when I left for Romania and that wasn't easy.

Ailbhe and Neasa, our pride and joy.

Bertie won the election! And we won the match.

ENGLAND BEATEN AGAIN!

ANOTHER SEASON dawned with not just the public but ourselves as well wondering if we could recapture the spirit and camaraderie and friendship that had been such important elements of our success in Europe over the years. We had gone so close and not quite made it that we could hardly complain if our supporters were becoming just a little frustrated and if we were honest with ourselves, the fear was in our own minds that we might never see the big days again.

We got a decent enough draw, Castres against whom we had struggled in the past, Harlequins with their long list of cosmopolitan stars and Bridgend from Wales. Getting the players fired up wasn't a problem but we still had to watch our backs at home while picking something up away.

But there was more than Munster to worry about. We had the hangover"foot and mouth"Internationals and the Celtic League. There was going to be a lot of rugby before Christmas. An Irish squad was picked for the Scottish match and everybody wanted to be involved because we had beaten Italy and France and there was a lot to be played for where the Six Nations Championship was concerned.

But then I got the dreaded phone call from Briano. I was on the way back from Kerry on my own when the phone rang. The penny didn't drop with me for a while as we chatted but eventually he told he was the bearer of bad news. The first thing that entered my mind was whether I was out of the squad or out of the team. I had known Briano since 1985 when I joined Shannon and had worked closely with him at club, provincial and international level. It was the first time he had given me bad news - I was out of the team and squad, something like the eleventh time I had been dropped by Ireland.

I was very disappointed. Brian rang me again that evening and said that Joan would kill him. Gatland had offered to do it but Brian said he'd face the music himself. It was that time above all other times that I felt it was going to be very hard to come back. I won't say I threw in the towel but Warren had been saying at the time that they had to build for the World Cup. Jeremy Davidson and Malcolm O'Kelly were in the side and Gary Longwell on the bench. No doubt about it, three good players so I felt this might be the end. It wasn't the end I wanted. It looked like my last match had been as captain in Romania and that was some consolation.

Joan tried to buck me up but I was moping around the house. The kids were crying and I wasn't paying too much attention. She told me to snap out of it, that it wasn't the end of the world. I had plenty of practice at being dropped but when I was dropped before I could see a way back. When I was dropped before it was probably because they felt I wasn't good enough. Now I was being told that along with being also told that I was too old. Briano assured me there was a way back but I couldn't see it.

Then came the Scottish match and it was nothing short of a disaster. I was on RTE the same day as a panellist and when it was over Tom McGurk put it to me that there would be a lot of people down in Limerick and even myself happy at the result and the way the team had played. But that was not the case. Definitely not. At the end of the day I was a member of a squad that had been unbeaten in the Six Nations and now the Triple Crown and the Grand Slam were gone out the window. You don't get too many chances where they are concerned. I was genuinely disappointed.

After that, there was a hue and cry to bring me back and I wondered if that would work for or against me. Munster had already beaten Castres in the Heineken Cup and now we had another game against Harlequins at The Stoop between the Scotland and Wales games and I suppose I saw it as both an opportunity to get back on the Irish team and more importantly to keep the Munster show on the road. Woody was there and they had a crack side and after a slow start we showed some of the old flair, won with plenty to spare and a lot of fellas were rewarded when the Irish squad was announce, myself included.

There were a number of changes for the Wales game. David Wallace and Peter Stringer had been dropped along with myself and they were brought back as well into the team. Gary Longwell and myself were in the second-row and Malcolm was dropped but it was one of the shortest droppings of all time. He was dropped at five to ten but within an hour Gary had broken his finger and was out again. A win and nothing else would suffice in Cardiff and everything went our way on the day. David Wallace and Peter Stringer made a point and even Claw produced a great run up the middle of the field. It was great to be back in a winning Irish jersey and it was a thrill to play in the Millennium Stadium.

Then we were preparing for England's visit to Dublin in pursuit of the Grand Slam. Scotland had foiled them two years previously, Wales had done it the year before and now it was up to us. Stopping England winning the slam and the crown would have been seen as being as good as winning them ourselves. They came as hot favourites but they came without the injured Martin Johnson and he was a big loss. The players genuinely felt we had a chance. It was a perfect day for rugby, there was a good build-up. Frankie, Rog and myself went out for lunch on the Friday. It's great to walk down Grafton Street and have people shouting good luck to-morrow and that kind of thing. Far better than being stuck in the hotel all the time, there's a real feel good factor about it.

Equally, on the day of the game, it fires you up to walk through the lobby in the Berkley Court and hear all the good wishes, it gives you an additional gee up. For some reason, we turn left out of the Berkley Court and go down to Jurys corner and around by the pubs. We turn a two minute journey into a six minue journey and it adds to the atmosphere. We all sit in the same place. Claw, Anthony and myself are always in the back seat, be it for Ireland or Munster. I suppose the more experienced you become, the further back you go. I wouldn't be superstitious but if I saw a magpie on the road I'd be looking out for the second fella. If I didn't see him I'd salute the first fella, if you're friendly with him, it's kind of o.k., there's no element of bad luck any more! I notice Ronan is moving ever nearer to the back of the bus, he's becoming one of the big boys.

Our custom is to get to the ground an hour before the kick-off. Mikey

Mullins had chosen the music over the p.a., U2 and that kind of stuff, and it sounded good as we had our walk around the pitch. Our gut feeling was that we were going to do well. We knew how important it was and how big a prize it was to beat England, one of the best teams in the world. We had played the two previous matches whereas England were coming in cold and that definitely stood to us.

It was one of those great days in Lansdowne Road. Woody's try early on was something we had practised over and over again. Woody called it, a lob ball to me, I fed it to Anthony Foley and he popped it to Woody and he did the rest. That kind of thing works only once in a lifetime. As a professional rugby player, these are the things you practice all the time but it only takes one guy to be in the wrong position, or a crooked throw or a bad catch, to spoil it. There were five movements and everything went right and more importantly the opposition didn't get near it. That score gave us a great lift.

We'll always remember Stringer's ankle tap on Dan Luger. If that hadn't happened, it was curtains and I don't think anybody else could have carried it off. That lifted us at a time when we were only just hanging in there. Then Claw and myself were brought off together and at that point we couldn't have been further from the dug out. It was really stage managed, the crowd went mad and gave us a standing ovation. That must have given the team an additional lift and Rog kicked another great penalty and we won a fantastic game.
Peter and I were lucky that we had beaten them in '93 and '94 and we had said to the lads beforehand that there was no better feeling in the game than beating England. We did the lap of honour around Lansdowne Road while they were getting their trophy, all of them with sullen faces. We had spoiled their party. Bertie Ahern was in the dressingroom afterwards and Briano sang Stand Up and Fight which, of course, is the Munster song. Coming off the pitch and going down the tunnel towards the dressing room, I made eye contact with Brian Ashton, now a part of the English coaching set-up but the only Irish coach never to pick me for Ireland. I said: "Well Brian how are things now" and he replied:- " Could be better". And I said: "I know the feeling". I'm not one to rub salt in wounds but that was too good a chance to miss!

To be part of beating England that late in my career having seen no way back only three weeks earlier was very satisfying. It's hard to say it was the highlight of my international career. 1993 and scoring the try against them was massive and going over to Twickenham the following year and beating them with good scores was also special. There were great players in all those teams.

The following week Munster played Bridgend in Wales in the next round of the Heineken Cup. John Kelly scored two tries that night but it was close and we were glad to get out with a win. Ireland then played Samoa and beat them well with Jeremy Staunton scoring a try on his debut. That reminded me of my first cap. There was a great crowd up from Galbally, just like half Castleisland seemed to be there on the day I first pulled on the jersey. GAA background people, if you like, and they were like a breath of fresh air. Anthony Foley was captain and got a bad knock in the face just before half time and had to go off. So I took over the captaincy and maybe that's why I was allowed to see out the end of the match, something that wasn't happening very often at this stage of my career.

Then it was on the following week to meet a New Zealand team coached by John Mitchell, whom I had played against for the Lions and also when he played for Garryowen. On the Sunday after Samoa, we went down to Aughrim for clay pigeon shooting but they wouldn't give the guns to Claw, Rog and myself and we went horse riding instead. We went up the side of a mountain and managed to come back in one piece. Later on, we had a nice dinner in Greystones and after that we were tired and felt like bed. But Briano urged us to come downstairs for a pint and who was below in the bar only Christy Moore. We had him to ourselves, thirty odd of us, he chatted away and sang songs and told a few stories. I'm a great fan of Christy and play his tapes all the time in the car. I remember John Hayes and myself had our picture taken with him and we presented him with an English jersey that Rala (Paddy O'Reilly, our fantastic bagman and the kind of fella the Irish soccer team could have done with in Saipan!) had and which was signed by the Irish team. It was a memento of the day we beat England and we knew Christy was a big rugby fan. It gave us all a great buzz.

We trained well for the New Zealand game and were really up for it. It was more or less the same side that beat England. We knew we had to perform even better than in that game and we did play well in the first half and were ahead at the break. We were matching them physically but let them in for an easy enough try just before half time. Denis Hickie scored shortly afterwards and we were really rolling. To be honest, if it was any other team, I believe we would have won that match. But the outcome showed me more about the All Blacks than ourselves. They had a comfortable win in the end and that was a huge disappointment for you don't have too many chances to beat New Zealand. It just went to show what a quality side they are. It was a chance to make history and we left it after us..

There was also the Celtic League to keep us occupied. We played Llanelli at Thomond Park in the quarter-final and it wasn't a classic but it was really tough. Peter Stringer couldn't play and Mikey Prendergast made a great replacement, scored a try and was voted man of the match. An indication, if you like, of the strength in the squad. From there it was on to what could best be described as a messy old match against Bridgend in the Heineken Cup at Musgrave Park. They were all over the place, fellas being sin binned and warned all the time, and one of them, threatened a touch judge, something I never saw previously. They lost their discipline completely and let themselves down.

We then beat Ulster in the semi-final of the Celtic League and at this point Stringer was injured again and Peter Clohessy had to revert to tight head for John Hayes who missed out on a few games. Marcus Horan came in at loose head. It wasn't a great game and was more a kicking duel between Ronan O'Gara and David Humphreys and Rog just came out on top.

That put us into the final against Leinster who were playing very well at the time and had a new belief in themselves. Stringer, Hayes and David Wallace were missing but in fairness, Leinster played very well and we didn't make the injuries an excuse. It was great to get to the final. I'm not making excuses but we had played a lot of rugby and Leinster were fresher and reacted better. They got two good tries and outwitted us on the day. No Munster team likes to lose to Leinster and they'd be the same the other way around. Eric Miller got sent off but that seemed to bring them together even more and they deserved to win it on the day. It was another final defeat for Munster and while you wouldn't look at it as significant as a Heineken Cup final, it was a final defeat and it was against Leinster.

We had a meeting the following Monday. It wasn't a crisis meeting but we hadn't been performing and knew we had to change things if we wanted to come out of our group in the Heineken Cup. We needed to be fresher and Christmas was a welcome break. My only week-end off was the Scottish game and looking back I know now that I definitely needed a rest. I played around sixteen matches before Christmas and they were all competitive. After that, we had a Christmas party, paint balling down in Shanagolden and a bit of craic in Tralee. We were still a very proud team and there was still a lot of rugby to be played!

Myself, John Hayes and Frankie Sheahan.

Collecting the wrong trophy

RUGBY AND GAELIC FOOTBALL

IF I was giving a lot to rugby, it was giving a lot back to me. That's the thing about rugby, we travel to countries and places we would never otherwise have any chance of seeing. We meet all sorts of different people and get to understand their ways and in some cases make lifelong friendships.

That's a drawback about the GAA. I know the hurlers went to Argentina last year but that's a holiday more than anything else and not an occasion as such. More and more are headed all over the world nowadays but we do so as well to play for Ireland and there's a big difference between that and going on a holiday. It's a shame these lads can't ever really represent their country for they go through a lot and are wonderful sportsmen.

It's a joke, it's wrong that they're not being compensated for what they put into the games. You don't have to be a mathematician to work it out. It doesn't take a whole of money to pay players given the kind of money they're bringing in year after year. If it works in rugby, why can't it work in GAA? It's very strictly run in rugby and very professionally. People may claim there are too many players to pay in GAA so o.k., pay them for playing in the championships, pay them part time. There doesn't seem to be any will to do anything about it. They're boasting, actually boasting, about having the biggest attendances in the world and yet they're not giving anything to the players. Where else would you see it? They'll have to do something, bite the bullet and go for it.

Rugby, of course, is my game but I still have a very deep love, a Grá, for gaelic football. You talk about great scores in sport and shortly I'll move on to Brian O'Driscoll's famous try for the Lions in the first Aussie Test of 2001. But another score that will always live with me was Maurice Fitzgerald's point for Kerry against Dublin in Thurles the same summer. I have seen many amazing things in sport but his point from the sideline kick is up there with the best of them and beyond most. Pressure is the same in any game and there's no greater pressure than playing football for Kerry or hurling for Kilkenny or rugby for Munster.

We all have our own pressures. Where in the world would you go to see it.

Some great rugby players were lost in the Kerry team of the 70s. There was a position on the rugby field for everyone of them. Just think of it ... Bomber at number eight, Jack O'Shea at wing-forward and so on. Imagine Mikey Sheehy as an out-half. Paudie O'Shea played senior rugby with Young Munster. Funny, I played a charity rugby match one day in Castleisland and playing the same day were Charlie Nelligan, Tommy Doyle, Jim Deenihan, Ogie. You could see they were natural sportsmen and what wonderful rugby players they would have made.

It says a lot for how well Ireland does in rugby. Can you imagine an Irish team if we didn't have any GAA like, say, New Zealand, where every athlete is going to be available to play rugby. I think we'd be as good as any country and better than a lot of them. There's no reason why not. And they're still coming through year after year. Wouldn't you love to watch that little fella, Colin Cooper, operating these days in the corner for Kerry, on a rugby arena - the proverbial will-o'-the-wisp. If he can survive on a football pitch, he'll survive on a rugby pitch. He's probably the same size as Peter Stringer; if he got the proper training, he might even be bigger. But here's the difference again. Peter would probably be as hard as nails anyway but he has been properly trained. If Cooper was put on a good weights programme, you can only imagine how he would fill out.

Having come back from Romania, with the arrival of the new baby, it was a big change from having one child to two. But it was a great joy and another great highlight of my life. Around that time, too, I had an operation on my leg. I had taken a bad kick on the shin and it was flaring up all the time. I had to get all the veins stripped out. Paul O'Byrne who was involved with Garryowen and played with Connacht did the job. It was great to have a rugbyman who knew the scene looking after affairs.

It meant I couldn't go to Poland with the Irish squad and as you can imagine that broke my heart! That kind of training is great for the younger guys but for fellas like myself and the Claw, it was a bridge too far. He didn't go either. That therapy can be good but the most I have ever done is to get into a cold bath for three minutes, it's very good for recovery after a match and helps to drop the body temperature.

Instead I went off to Australia and the Lions tour with a bunch of lads. I had been a playing member of a Lions tour in 1993 but things had moved on the hell of a lot by then. The 1997 tour of South Africa gave the Lions a huge profile and this one, so they thought, was going to be even better. There was a great atmosphere. Everybody loves the Irish and we enjoyed ourselves. The first Test was in the Gabba and Woody was playing, Brian O'Driscoll and Rob Henderson, who we knew was coming to Munster the following season. It was great to be there that night and see the try that Brian got. It was fantastic, top drawer stuff. Everybody still talks about that try but to have been there in person to see it was unbelievable. 'Twas nice to be able to say I played with him a couple of months ago. You see talented players and Brian really fits the bill. What's more important, he's a nice fella, you can be very talented and still be a nice guy. That's why I admire him so much. Recovering from the operation and going on that tour whetted my appetite once again for rugby. Talking rugby instead of playing it was terrific and, of course, like any man away, I had a good few pints, but already I was thinking about getting back into training. That was one of the many good things that came out of that trip. Little did I know that another memorable if bitter-sweet season lay ahead!

Seamus Moynihan, Captain of the Kerry Team 2000 and myself.

Peter went up to the referee and said, “He bit me”.

THE LASSISSI AFFAIR!

WE GAVE Harlequins a bit of a hiding at Thomond Park when the Heineken Cup resumed shortly after Christmas and that guaranteed us a place in the quarter-final. To make sure of the home draw, though, we had to get something out of our visit to Castres and that's an occasion none of us will ever forget. We didn't play anything like we had against Harlequins the previous week but even that pales into insignificance compared with the Claw-Lassissi affair.

Facts are facts. Claw was bitten. There are no two ways about it. He didn't do it himself. Afterwards, they tried to make out it wasn't a human bite. Peter went up to the referee and said he bit me. I saw it clearly for myself. You know teeth marks when you see them. The referee claimed he didn't see anything, his touch judges didn't see anything and so they insisted they couldn't react to what we said was a bite. Going by the law, he couldn't do anything in those circumstances. He called myself and Gregor Townsend, the Castres captain, together and told us to sort this out.

But Townsend went on about racist remarks which to us wasn't an issue. The issue was that Peter was bitten. He was just describing the fella. It wasn't in any way racist or anything like that. He was just telling the ref about the guy who had bitten him. He said something like the black f***** bit me. But there were fifteen of them and only one black fella and that was Peter's way of getting his message across. That's what all the hullaballoo was about afterwards which was very unfair on Peter because it wasn't a racist remark. It was purely a means of identification. If somebody bit me, no matter what colour or creed he was, I'm not too sure what I would call him but I wouldn't be thinking straight anyway, let's put it that way. Nobody likes citing a player but because of the nature of the incident, we had to do it. If we didn't, we would be seen to be condoning it and that was the way we felt about it.

It was all blown up after the match. Doctors came in and nobody was suggesting it wasn't a bite. Munster cited Lassissi which we had to do and Castres in turn cited Peter for this racism lark which really was a joke. Television showed it over and over again and it was clearcut as to who did it. It took over from what happened in the match itself, that we had lost in the last minute and we would be away in the quarter-final.

But it meant we had to go to Dublin and the ERC for the hearing. Peter and I went up, Jerry Holland and the team doctor Michael Shinkwin were there and they were called in. I wasn't called. The case against Peter was dropped and Lassissi got the minimum suspension of one year. That seemed to be the end of that and we were reasonably happy that justice had been served even if we still resented the fact that Peter's name and Munster's impeccable and justified reputation for fair and sporting play had been dragged through the mud.

The loss in Castres meant we had to travel to Stade Francais. That was a huge ask for us because they had beaten us in Lille the previous year in the semi-final and seemed to have all the aces. They hadn't been beaten on their own ground for ages, they had hammered teams there and were something like ourselves in Thomond Park where keeping an unbeaten record was concerned.

Everything was going fine from our point of view. We were over in France and the last thing in our minds was the Lassissi affair. We thought it had all been put to bed. But we were wrong. An appeal was heard in Dublin on the Thursday. They brought over their specialists and basically he got away with it. The news came through but to be honest, it didn't bother the team, we had done what we had to do and it was out of our hands.

We just wanted to concentrate on the Stade Francais match. We went to the Stade Jean Bouin on the Thursday and felt it was a lovely ground. I remember having played on the same pitch the time Shannon went over there around 1987 or '88 to take on Toulon. It's in the shadow of the Parc de Prince and a lovely place, really. There was a massive crowd and as usual it was hard to get tickets, another amazing situation really given the expense and how little time the fans had to organise things.

There was a howling wind blowing down the middle of the pitch, undoubtedly the strongest I ever came up against in my career. We lost the toss and they gave us the wind and it was some wind. It was a hard, physical match and as fast as any International. Come to think of it, they all are at that stage of the Heineken Cup, there's hardly any difference. The pace is no different, the hits are just as hard and come just as quick. Just look at Stade Francais, they have a full International team drawn from all over the rugby world. They were a real cosmopolitan outfit.

Anthony Horgan got a great try that day, he ran right through the middle of their defence and we led 16-0 at half time. They got it back to 16-14 with a soft try and Diego Dominguez kicked a few penalties but crucially he missed the conversion. Our defence was superb all day but somehow we left them through a maul near the line which should have been bread and butter stuff to us. For the last fifteen minutes, we didn't give away a penalty inside our own half. Come to think of it, we had to be careful almost anywhere within seventy yards of the posts for Dominguez is a huge kicker of the ball and we felt he could put one over from almost anywhere.

We showed great discipline. It wasn't just a case of holding on to the ball, it was more a case of not giving away penalties. Jim Williams, David Wallace and Anthony Foley did a great job in the back-row. Paul O'Connell had a huge game in the second-row and came of age against the French International Aradou. Paul was head and shoulders above the rest, I had helped him along the way, he was a fella who burst on to the Munster scene and quickly made a name for himself. He's a fantastic prospect although he has been very unfortunate in the way of injuries.

In truth, everybody played well that day and we pulled off one of the most satisfying of all our victories. That result was really against the head. At that point Declan and Niallo were on their way to Ireland having taken over from Warren Gatland, about which more later, and one thing was very much in the backs of our minds. If we lost, our season was over and that wasn't the way we wanted it to end. We would have been splitting up at the end of January. I think this was one of our finest performances, real backs to the wall stuff. We showed a level of maturity we probably hadn't seen before. We always played with our hearts but we played with our heads as well that day

It took me over twenty minutes to get off the pitch there were so many Munster supporters there. I had friends from Castleisland and all sorts of places and they were swinging out of me and the smell of drink was ridiculous, I'll never forget it. It was like going from a rugby match to a rock festival. We only knew two weeks previously that we were going there and while that was fine for the team, for the supporters it meant making hasty arrangements and digging deep into their pockets again and again and again.

We went to a reception in the Parc des Princes and to have won in the shadow of the place helped in a small way to exorcise all the ghosts of Irish hammerings there over the years. If we had lost, it would have been my last game as captain, Peter's last game for Munster, the end of an era, and we didn't want it to end in Paris. It was something we were all conscious of but we never talked about that or that Declan and Niallo were leaving. We never made it a motivational factor, yet 'twas there in the backs of all our minds.

Anthony Horgan scores the crucial try.

The Before and After

The final words in the huddle

We know how to celebrate

Paul O'Connell grabs another one

WARREN OUT, EDDIE IN

WE WERE now back into the International arena and were going there without Warren Gatland, who had been sacked the previous December and replaced with a team led by Eddie O'Sullivan as coach and Declan Kidney and Niall O'Donovan as assistant coach and forwards coach respectively. Warren's departure came as a big shock at the time. The perception was that he might have been under pressure after the Scottish game but we turned around and beat Wales, England and Samoa and were unlucky not to beat the All Blacks.

Many people would have been happy with that track record but whatever happened between Warren and the IRFU, he didn't have his contract. He might have called it on himself to a certain extent by asking for an earlier renewal but it wasn't something the players had expected, it came out of the blue. It came as a bit of a shock to the system. The timing seemed strange. I felt sorry for Warren. Whether you're a player or coach, I'm sure it feels the same. I suppose I feel sorry for anybody in those circumstances. At the same time, I was delighted for Niallo and Declan and for Eddie who also put a lot of work in.

It was one of those matters in which the players couldn't get involved. We just had to put our shoulder to the wheel and work even harder because there was a new coach. Players come and go but when coaches come and go, it's different. It was a major talking point at the time and probably still is. It will always raise its head when Ireland are playing.

I didn't know what repercussions there would be for me from the change. I was now heading for 36 and fully appreciated that they would be looking for younger blood, especially with the World Cup looming in eighteen months or so. Obviously it was going to put pressure on Declan and Niallo but at the same time I knew Eddie was the boss. He came to me and spoke to me. I wanted to know what he expected of me and I told him what I wanted and that was to keep going to see out the year.

In fairness to Eddie, he told me I'd get my opportunities. He was very fair and blunt about it. If things go well, you'll be fine, was the message but if not, then he'd be looking for a younger man. That was fine by me for he had to be seen to be looking to the future and that had been the case as well in Warren's time so I knew where I stood. The most important thing was for me to maintain my form and continue to play well.

Our first game was against Wales at Lansdowne Road and we hammered them. There were seven Munster fellas in the pack and Paul O'Connell got the call after his blinder against Stade Francais the previous week and got a try on his debut which was obviously a great thrill for him. It was also great for me because Woody was out with injury and it was my first time to captain Ireland at Lansdowne Road in a Six Nations match. It was nice to get the chance against Romania but that was in front of a few hundred people in the middle of nowhere but it was fantastic to do the job at Lansdowne and win the game. That was the most important thing.

We had been expecting a backlash from the Welsh but with so many Munster players in the side, we were able to pick up where we left off against Stade Francais. I don't know whether he was naive or what but Paul O'Connell went to tackle Scott Quinnell and he got an elbow and shoulder in the head. He was caught off guard and was all over the place. We knew he was in trouble, probably concussed. He asked me the calls at one stage and then we knew for sure. I had often been concussed myself and so I knew what was happening. It's an awful thing for a minute after taking the bang, you have no memory of the present. He scored a great try but couldn't remember it.

We were having a five man line-out and I asked Paul if he was ready for it and he said he wasn't. The next thing he told me was "I'm out of here" and of course I told him he couldn't go then, not in the middle of a line-out. But he said, "I don't know what's happening, I'm out of here", and just walked off the pitch. And there we were in the middle of Lansdowne Road playing Wales in the Six Nations, we had called a move and it was supposed to involve Paul.

Anyway, we beat the Welsh easily and after that it was on to Twickenham and what we knew was going to be a massive test against England. It was only natural that they would be looking for revenge for the defeat back in October and we knew they would come at us with all barrels blazing in the early stages. Somehow we kept them at 6-3 for a while but inevitably the floodgates opened and we were ripped apart. Then we gave them a soft try after half time. They were on their way to a huge victory and one that rocked us back on our heels.

I was taken off about fifteen minutes after half time and as I walked away I was wondering if this was it, was this my Ireland career over and if so, it was an awful way to go. 'Twas desperate, we were back to square one after putting a record score on Wales and now England had put a record score on us. Two weeks was a long time in rugby. In fairness to England, they weren't gloating but you could see they were very happy. I think the stats came out that night and showed England as the number one team in the world, they had passed out the other big guns from Australia and New Zealand and they were very chuffed about that. It's funny the way things go, two weeks later England went over to Paris and France beat them. People had been saying there was no one to touch England but France proved otherwise and that's the great thing about sport.

After the England debacle, I was wondering what was going to happen. The dogs in the street knew that we hadn't played well and personally I didn't play well. I asked Eddie straight out what he was going to do and he replied that he hadn't made his mind up. We were coming together on the following Monday week and on the previous day Eddie told me we'd all be there for the Scotland game. I was delighted with that. What's more, I was still captain so we had a chat about getting the thing back on the rails. It had been a brave call not to drop anyone after Twickenham but now we had to repay Eddie and the boys with a win over the Scots, who had always given Ireland a lot of trouble and had actually beaten them the previous October.

We performed well and put a record score on the Scots and that was a great relief. Everybody played up to scratch and Brian O'Driscoll had a seriously big match. I came off and Keith Gleeson came on for his first cap and went on to score a try but I got the by now usual standing ovation as I walked off. I felt the whole thing was back on track and as captain I was especially delighted. Little did I know at the time that it would be my last cap although if ever there was a good game to go out on, then it was captaining Ireland to beat Scotland at Lansdowne Road. We always had a lot of trouble agains them and I have won more times against England than I have against the Scots.

I just didn't see it coming this time although I was always wary. We had a three day squad session up in Belfast which went very well until I again got the dreaded phone call from Briano. I said, Jeez, not again. I went up to his room and Briano and Eddie were there and I asked, what's the story this time, and they said they wanted to go with Gary Longwell. I didn't argue, a done deal is a done deal, and I thanked them for the past few matches. It was pointless going on about the ifs and buts, I've never argued with selectors why this or why that. If they wanted to explain to me, fine, if not, that's o.k. too. I think this was the twelfth time I had been dropped and I knew unless there were a lot of injuries, this was the end.

I kept it to myself on the bus on the way down. Cheltenham was on at the time, Frankie and I had a few bob on Florida Pearl and out of loyalty I put a few bob on Istabraq as well. We went into the airport hotel bar to watch the racing, some were flying back to Cork, some to Shannon, I was driving to Kilkenny and as we went our separate ways the boys said we'll see you next week. But I said that I wouldn't, I told them I was gone and they were clearly shocked. But what do you say to a fella who's been dropped? It was something that I had to get on with. One of the Kerry papers said 'twas a good and a bad day for the county. Jim Cullotty was the jockey of the Gold Cup winner Best Mate and Mick Galway was dropped as Irish captain. The same day, as well, Istqbraq retired so the slags had it that Istabraq and Galwey were put out to grass together. The lousers were comparing me to a horse in one of my darkest moments!

Woody was back as captain and I went to the match with a friend of mine, Sean Dunne. Ireland beat Italy handy enough and I didn't hang around afterwards. In the past, people would always say you'll be back, you'll be back but when they said it this time, I knew damn well there was no hope. I was O.K. If somebody told me I'd captain Ireland four times and have only one loss which isn't a bad return, I'd have been glad to believe them. It was something I had always wanted to do.

According to the records, I've done this 85 times.

The Celebration: Killian Keane, Eddie Halvey and Dominic Crotty

CASTRES AGAIN!

BUT THE season wasn't over, not by a long shot. I travelled over to Cardiff for the Heineken Cup semi-final draw and typical of Leicester's luck, their name came out of the hat first against Llanelli. There were a lot of Llanelli people there and I knew they wanted a Munster-Llanelli final at the Millennium Stadium.

Then Castres were pulled out and, boy, did that give us a sinking feel for it meant that once again we were away to a French team in the semi-final of the Heineken Cup. It was a disaster for our supporters and it got worse when they started talking about Beziers in the deep south as the likely venue. We pointed out where that was and how difficult it would be for our supporters to get there. I know that Lille the previous year was a disaster because it's not a rugby stronghold but at least they were getting that part right on this occasion. Looking back, it worked out very well and it was a lovely place.

The boys had come through the Six Nations and the last thing we wanted was injuries. Worst of all, though, was Peter Clohessy's accident at home when he burned himself pretty badly and looked certain to miss the match. But he worked like nobody else could to make it and it was his courage and determination that enabled him to complete a miraculous recovery.

Our all consuming ambition was to get back into the final but we got a bit of a shock when the team arrived on Thursday and we were hit by this vicious blast of heat and we arrived there around kick-off time, 3 o'clock, so we didn't like that very much. We took over this massive guesthouse that we had all to ourselves. We had a chef who followed us around wherever we went because he knew what we wanted. All the stuff we needed, Tipperary water, potatoes, beans, stuff like that. The gear went there with Noel Healy, the "Budda" himself. The team was a passion with him and he just wanted to do it. We were training in Cork on the Tuesday and he took off with it all by road.

Luckily, it got a little cooler the following day. By this time we were taking in water like it was going out of fashion. The fact that we had the place to ourselves meant we could concentrate exclusively on rugby. That night we went into Montpellier, a lovely city, walked through the streets and we saw the bars and our fans singing their songs, the Isle, Beautiful Munsters, Hurrah for Garryowen, the Cons are here, all the songs and it was terrific to see and hear.

It just proved that the whole Munster thing had pulled everybody together. We all have our strong club loyalties but everybody got behind Munster which wasn't the case in years gone by and that made us very proud. It was great to see the masses of people having a great time and having the craic. I think there was something like 10, 000 people down there, it was quite amazing.

We had taken the cold baths and drunk all the water to cope with the heat. We had prepared well for this one. The previous time Castres beat us, they beat us up front and again we started badly. Lassissi, of course, was playing. Everybody was expecting a big clash between himself and the Claw but it was never an issue that day. It was a hard, physical game, as hard as we have played, and we were 12-3 down approaching half time but playing against a strong wind. But we came back and it was 12-9 at half time and we were very happy to settle for that. They had played all the rugby but we were only three points behind turning to play with the breeze.

We came out to see a sea of red at one end and a sea of blue at the other and I felt that was a pity in a way. What harm would it have done to mix them up. Also, there was a bitter rivalry between Beziers and Castres. Beziers played in red and they sported their jerseys that day! So the support was there for us and we weren't going to let them down. We played a solid game and our defence was good. I know we let them in for a try at the end but John Kelly got a great breakaway try, Ronan had a huge game, Alan Quinlan did very well, so it was great to reward our supporters.

But the star of the show was Donnacha O'Callaghan. Anthony Foley injured his shoulder early on tackling Lassissi and Donnacha came on and played a huge match, he was all over the place. He came of age that day. The previous year against Stade Francais he played at wing-forward and it hadn't gone very well for him. This time was different. He was fantastic, he led from the front and some of his drives were inspirational and it was great for the team to see that happen.

A funny incident was the time the Claw and the Castres South African prop Moyle were sin binned. They sat on the same bench and Peter was chatting away to him. Afterwards we asked him what they were saying to each other. Peter said to him, if you were any good, you'd still be back in South Africa and your man turned around to Peter and asked how often Ireland had beaten South Africa. In reply, Peter squirted water all over him!

At the final whistle we got into a huddle in the middle of the pitch and I told the lads we were back where we wanted to be. Let's make sure that everything is geared towards the final and there must be no distractions. It's going to be a massive scene in the Millennium Stadium.

There was a lot of rough handling of our supporters. As with the Stade Francais game, they probably thought they could come on to the pitch and I think we wanted that as well. But the security there was very heavy handed. They knocked Munster fans to the ground with rugby tackles and one guy broke his collar bone. The stewards lost it completely. We did our lap of honour. Days like that are great, that's why you play the game. There were no major injuries and the following day we saw Leicester beating Llanelli at the Nottingham Forest football ground.

In many ways, I wanted Llanelli to win. However, had they done so, there wouldn't have been a ticket to be had and we wouldn't have the Welsh crowd behind us in the final. Twasn't that I didn't want to meet Leicester but I knew it would be a massive ask to beat them in a Heineken Cup final. They got through with a massive kick by Tim Stimpson right at the end. I felt so sorry for Llaneli, they had played all the rugby and were a side who deserved to be in a Heineken Cup final. Like ourselves, they came from a country area, they wouldn't have the big spending power of Leicester and others like that.

Once again we had a ticket fiasco leading up to the final. People got there every way they could. We kept a lower profile than we had two years previously. True, we did have our public relation days in Thomond Park and Musgrave Park which always went great and it was nice for the kids to come along and get their autographs and so on. In preparation, we also played an Interpro against Ulster in Ravenhill and it didn't go well for us. They were up for it and played well on the night. There were some good aspects to our game, it's just that the urgency wasn't there but it was something we didn't worry about because we knew it would be there for the final.

The pressure was huge but this was somewhere we wanted to be and these are things you have to be able to handle. The whole country was behind us. We flew out on the Thursday and stayed in the Vale of Glamorgan and did our usual run around and stretches. It was an indoor arena belonging to the Welsh Rugby Union and we had a game of tip rugby. In all the toing and froing, Anthony Horgan got his thumb in somebody's togs and broke it. It was freakish. How could that happen, we asked ourselves. Everybody had put their body on the line against Castres and nobody got injured.

I felt very disappointed for Anthony because he had also been chosen for the Irish tour of New Zealand. John O'Neill came in and gave the team a great lift but for Hoggy it was a disaster. It wasn't the kind of situation you wanted to be in the day before a final.

At the press conference, Leicester tried to put the heat on us but everybody knew they had to be favourites. There was a great Munster crowd around, families and so on. Neasa and Ailbhe came out on the pitch and we had photgraphs taken. That's the kind of set-up Munster is, the families are very important and Declan worked very hard on that side of the thing. Our families weren't staying with us, they were in Cardiff itself. Everybody in Wales seemed to be for us and they gave us the favoured home dressingroom. Not that we cared one way or the other, a dressingroom isn't going to win a game for you and as it turned out, it didn't do us any good.
Martin Johnson and I were photographed looking down on the pitch and I was thinking to myself, if I was a supporter at this match, I'd be

so emotional and carried away. I thought of how lucky I was and how lucky we all were to be playing in front of a full house in this stadium the following day. It is a fabulous stadium. You can talk about a lot of other stadiums, Twickenham, wherever, but for me this is the very best, the place you want to play in, if only for the atmosphere alone.

Chatting among ourselves on the Friday night, we were conscious that this could be the end of an era. Driving to the ground on Cardiff was amazing. I had played many matches in Cardiff but I never saw anything like the number of people. The sea of red was amazing. We didn't go straight to the ground, we drove around town to get into the atmosphere. I remember seeing John "Pako" Fitzgerald standing outside a pub and he gave us a clenched fist salute as only he could. It was clear to see how proud he was and it was great to see a former player so supportive. He's just one of many who stands out in my memory. My own mother was there, she had been in Twickenham two years previously and hadn't been very far in the meantime. My three sisters and brother came home from America, Joan most of her family and the girls were there, all my friends from Kerry, Limerick, Kilkenny and so on were there.

We felt we had it right. We were nervous as hell and, of course, they decided to close the roof but that didn't matter to us because it was the same for both sides. The one mistake they made was in trying to create an atmosphere through music which they didn't need to do because the Munster crowd would have sung anyway. Twas like being in a disco. Out we came and there must have been 40, 000 there from Munster and the Welsh people were wearing their national jerseys so we knew who they were cheering for as well.

The rest, as they say, is history, we lost on that faithful day in Cardiff.

A new season, 2002/'03, has begun and a new management and captain are in place. I'm still playing and I hope Jim Williams, Alan Gaffney and Brian Hickey get a flavour of all the wonderful times we've had in the Heineken Cup.

Bank of Ireland

EPILOGUE

MY WIFE Joan has been my strongest support and greatest critic - from counting the number of times I say, "at the end of the day" in interviews to giving me a much needed reality check when rugby might have been getting me down. I can always count on her.

It's not easy being married to a rugby player. Joan often says it's like being a second-class citizen in your own home as diet, rest, matches and recovery all take precedence. If they didn't, I wouldn't be playing into my 37th year. In the early professional days, Declan Kidney once told us that rest was more important than training. She says it was the worst thing I could have heard because I took it to heart so much! I have to be honest and admit I like nothing better than putting the feet up at home with the tv zapper at my side, sharing the telly time with Neasa and Ailbhe when Barney and their other favourites are on the box.

Joan has brought the children to Limerick, Cork, Dublin, London, Cardiff, Paris, even Boston and Toronto. People sometimes might look at Neasa and Ailbhe and wonder why we bother. It would be so much easier and often more enjoyable to leave them at home. There are two reasons. We want both of them to grow up knowing they were part of this great phenomenon called Munster rugby. Although Neasa will have much bigger crises in her life than the current "who took Daddy's number four jersey?" and Ailbhe is still too young to understand, we hope they will grow up feeling privileged like we do to have been part of it all. Secondly, being a professional rugby player involves a lot of time away from home. If we didn't bring them to matches, our contact time with them would be very limited.

I've enjoyed many famous moments on the playing fields of Ireland and the world and I will forever carry the memories of those great times with me. However, at the end of the day (sorry Joan!), the love and support of one's family supercedes all. In this regard, Joan has been a pillar whether times were good or bad. She was there for me through thick and thin since we first met in Woody's night club in Castleisland. Her love has been unstinting. We have been blessed with two lovely girls and, God willing, there will be a third member of the family before the end of the 2002/'03 rugby season!

My mother Bridget has to be my number one fan. There was never a time when I deserved to be dropped and to this day, it's woe betide anybody who criticises me. That's a mother's role, isn't it! Although her rugby following days have been curtailed in recent years due to her poor eyesight, she is totally in tune with the world of rugby from her kitchen in Currow. She listens to all the news reports and takes the disappointments worse than I do. She raised eight children and buried two husbands. I hope I have her will to live and ability to enjoy life at her age.

Last year, an elderly Kerry football supporter remarked to a friend of mine, "Mick Galwey was a great footballer but the rugby ruined him!" Everybody has their own perspective and for me two roads often diverge in a wood. There were several times through the years when I was tempted to throw in the towel but didn't. I have long dreaded the day when I wouldn't be able to run on to the pitch to the roar of the crowd and compete at the highest level.

That day is fast approaching. I look at the younger lads in the prime of their playing careers and envy them. What I wouldn't give to be starting again. I love this game. It has been very good to me. It gave me an education, a confidence I never had and brought me in contact with some of the greatest friends and nicest people one could meet. Whether I was or wasn't picked is now largely irrelevant. Winning is the easy part, it's how you cope with the knocks that counts. That's what builds character.

Rugby is like life. There's nothing fair about it. I have played with and against several players who deserved to be capped and never were. Lady luck and the hand of God play a huge part in all our lives. I think of my father who died at 48 and never saw me in a red or green jersey. I look at my family and know how much he would have adored them.
What the game gave me far, far outweighs whatever contribution I might have made. I can honestly say that I will look back in years to come and say "I was there and I loved it".

IRISH
PERMANENT

MICK GALWEY PLAYER STATISTICS

All statistics compiled by Des Daly, Irish Rugby Statistician

APPENDIX ONE
CAREER / HONOURS AT INTERNATIONAL LEVEL
ALL STATISTICS UP TO 01/08/2002

1987/88	Ireland "Shamrocks" tour (played in two of the four games) to France (5/88).
1988/89	IRE U-25 (bench only) v IT (12/88); Comb. Provs. v IT (1/89);
1989/90	Ireland tour to Canada and USA, 9/89 (not selected); IRE B v SCOT (12/89); IRE U-25 v USA (3 / 90); IRE (bench only) v WAL (3 / 90).
1990/91	IRE U-25 v SPAIN (9/90); IRE B v ARG (10/90); IRE B v SCOT (12/90); IRE v FRA (2/91); IRE v WAL (2/91); IRE B v ENG (3/91); Ireland tour (played in three of the four games) to Namibia, IRE – 2 (rep) v NAM (7/91).
1991/92	Ireland squad to second RWC; IRE v JAP (10/91); IRE v ENG (2/92); IRE v SCOT (2/92); IRE v FRA (3/92); Ireland tour (played in six of the eight games) to NZ, IRE – 1 v NZ (5/92); IRE –2 v NZ (6/92).
1992/93	IRE v AUS (10/92); Irish Final Trial (1/93); IRE V FRA (2/93); IRE v WAL (3/93); IRE v ENG, try-1, (3/93): IRE SEVENS to Hong Kong (3/93) and to RWC SEVENS, Edinburgh (4/93): British and Irish Lions tour to NZ (Summer 1993, played in seven of the 12 games, no test matches).

1993/94	IRE v ROM (11/93); IRE v FRA (1/94); IRE v WAL (2/94); IRE v ENG (2/94); IRE v SCOT (3/94); Ireland tour (eight games, played in four, one as captain) to AUS, IRE-1 v AUS (6/94).
1994/95	IRE DEVEL. XV v USA (11/94); IRE (rep) v USA (11/94); Comb. Provs. v SA (11/94); IRE v ENG (1/95); IRE A v WAL (3/95).
1995/96	Ireland squad to third RWC (not selected).
1996/97	IRE v W. SAMOA (11/96); IRE A (captain) v FRA (1/97); IRE A (captain) v WAL (1/97) (captain).
1997/98	IRE A v SCOT (2/98); IRE (rep) v FRA (3/98); Ireland tour to South Africa, 6/98 (seven games, played in two, one as captain).
1998/99	Comb. Provs. (captain) v SA (11/98); IRE A (captain) v SA (12/98); IRE (rep) v WAL (2/99); IRE A (captain) v IT (4/99); Ireland tour to Australia, 6/99 (not selected).
1999/2K	Ireland squad to fourth RWC (not selected); IRE (rep) v ENG, try –2, (2/2K); IRE v SCOT (2/2K); IRE v IT (3/2K); IRE v FRA (3/2K); IRE v WAL (4/2K); Ireland tour (played in two of the three games) to Americas, IRE v ARG (6/2K); IRE v CAN (6/2K).
2K/2001	IRE v IT (2 / 01) ; IRE v FRA (2 / 01) ; IRE v ROM. (6/ 01) (captain) try – 3 ; IRE v WAL (10 / 01) ; IRE v ENG (10 / 01).
2001/02	IRE v SAMOA (11 / 01); IRE v NZ (11 / 01) ; IRE v WAL (2 / 02) (captain); IRE v ENG (2 / 02) (captain) ; IRE v SCOT (3 / 02) (captain).

LEDGEND :

FRA	FRANCE	SCOT	SCOTLAND
CAN	CANADA	WAL	WALES
NZ	NEW ZEALAND	ARG	ARGENTINA
NAM	NAMIBIA	AUS	AUSTRALIA
WS	WESTERN SAMOA	JAP	JAPAN
ROM	ROMANIA	IT	ITALY
ENG	ENGLAND	RWC	RUGBY WORLD CUP

SUMMARY

- One Lions tour, six Ireland tours.
- Has 41 Ireland caps, (started 36 + 5 as replacement). Four times captain. Three Ireland tries.
- Ireland career: played 41, won 18, drawn 3, lost 20.
- Started 32 games as lock / 2nd row, two games as No. 6, two games as No. 8.
- Played seven games against England, France and Wales, four games against Scotland, three games against New Zealand, two games against Australia, Italy and Romania and once against Namibia, Japan, Western Samoa, USA, Argentina, Samoa and Canada.
- Most consecutive Ireland appearances: 9 - three in 1992 / 93 followed by six in 1993 / 94.
- Played in 13 non-test Ireland touring games, captain twice.
- Ten Ireland A / B caps, five times captain.
- Two Ireland U-25 caps; three Combined Provinces appearances, once as captain.
- One Ireland Development XV appearance.
- One Final Trial.

APPENDIX TWO

HONOURS AT (INTER)PROVINCIAL LEVEL

ALL STATISTICS UP TO 01 / 08 / 2002

		Caps
1987/88	C r.	1
1988/89	Llanelli, Pontypool, London and South East Division, C, U, Colunna-It	6
1989/90	Pontypool, L, C, U, New Zealand (L 9-31)(MP)	5
1990/91	Pontypool, C, U, L.	4
1991/92	No games – injured.	0
1992/93	Saracens, Irish Exiles, Pontypool, Australia, (W22-19) (MP) U, L, C.	7
1993/94	C, Scotish Exiles, L, Irish Exiles, Glasgow and District, U.	6
1994/95	U, Irish Exiles, L, C.	4
1995/96 -	Lombardi, Calvisano t, U, Irish Exiles, L,C*.	6
1996/97	Orrell, Ireland XV*, C*, L* 2t, U* t, Australia* (L 19-55) (TP)	6
1997/98	Edinburgh and District*, Caledonia Reds*, C* t, L*, U*.	5
1998/99	Llanelli* t n-c, C*, L*, U*, C*, U* t, L*.	6
1999/2K -	Dunvant*, L*, C*, U*, Ireland XV* (W 26-19) (MP), U*, L*, Leicester* n-c.	7

2K/2001	-	Glasgow Caledonians*, L'Aquila* n-c, U*, L*, C*, C*, U*, L*.	7
2001/02	-	Bath *, Edinburgh* (CL), C* (CL), Neath r t (CL), Newport* (CL), Cardiff* (CL) Llanelli* (QF-CL), U* (SF-CL), L* (F-CL), L*, U*.	11

			81

LEGEND:

*	Captain	n-c	non-capped game
MP	Musgrave Park	r	replacement
t	scored try	TP	Thomond Park
L	Leinster	U	Ulster
C	Connacht.	QF	quarter-final
CL	Celtic League	SF	semi-final
		F	final

SUMMARY

- Has played on six Munster sides that have won five Interprovincial Championships (including three Grand Slams) and one title share in the last nine seasons.
- Was captain on four title-winning occasions including the Grand Slams of 1996 / 97 and 1999 / 2000.
- The most-capped player in the Irish Interprovincial Championship (50 caps in 14 seasons).
- Has played 16 times against Ulster and Connacht, 14 times against Leinster, and has appeared in all four Munster outings against the Irish Exiles.
- Has missed out on only six Interprovincial games since he was first capped by Munster against Connacht in November 1987.
- Scored seven tries for Munster in non-European / Heineken Cup games.

APPENDIX THREE

HONOURS AT HEINEKEN CUP LEVEL

ALL STATISTICS UP TO 01 / 08 / 2002

		Caps
1995/96	SWANSEA (W17-13) (TP), CASTRES (L12-19) (A).	2
1996/97	MILAN (W23-5) (MP), CARDIFF (L18-48)(A), WASPS (W49-22) t (TP), TOULOUSE (L19-60) (A).	4
1997/98	HARLEQUINS (L40-48) t (A), CARDIFF (L23-43) (A), BOURGOIN (W17-15) (TP), CARDIFF (L32-37) (MP), BOURGOIN (L6-21) (A), HARLEQUINS (W23-16) (TP).	6
1998/99	PADOVA (W20-13) (MP), NEATH (W34-10) 2t (MP), PERPIGNAN (L24-41) t (A), NEATH (D18-18) t (A), PERPIGNAN (W13-5) (MP), PADOVA (W35-21) (A), COLOMIERS (QF, L9-23)(A).	7
1999/2K	PONTYPRIDD (W32-10) (TP), SARACENS (W35-34) (A), COLOMIERS (W31-15) (A), COLOMIERS (W23-5)(MP), SARACENS (W31-30) t (TP), PONTYPRIDD (L36- 38) (A), STADE FRANCAIS (QF, W27-10) (TP), TOULOUSE (SF, W31-25) (BORDEAUX), NORTHAMPTON (F, L 8-9) (TWICKENHAM).	9
2K/2001	NEWPORT (W26-18) t (TP), CASTRES (W32-29) (A), BATH (W31-9) (TP)*, BATH (L5- 18) (A), NEWPORT (W39-24) (A) , CASTRES (W21-11) (MP), BIARRITZ (QF, W38- 29) (TP) STADE FRANCAIS (SF, L 15-16) (LILLE).	8
2001/ 02	CASTRES (W28-23) (TP), HARLEQUINS (W24-8) (A),	

	Shannon; finishes season as the top try-scoring (16 tries) forward in the league after seven seasons.
1997/98	Munster Senior Cup medal (7); Shannon win fourth successive AIB title; plays in all 15 encounters and scores another six tries, including a hat-trick against O. Crescent.
1998/99	Plays in all eleven Shannon AIB games, scores two tries.
1999/2K	Munster Senior Cup medal (8); plays in eight of Shannon's eleven AIB outings, missing three games due to Munster's Heineken Cup successes.
2K/2001	Munster Senior Cup medal (9); marks his 100th AIB appearance with a try (his 25th AIB League try) against Terenure College on December 16th at Thomond Park.
2001 / 02	Shannon win their fifth AIB League title. Galwey plays in three of the 17 games including the semi-final and final play-offs; misses the Munster Senior Cup final due to preparations for the Heineken Cup final the following Saturday.

SUMMARY

- Has won five AIB League medals with Shannon in twelve seasons.
- Has won nine Munster Senior Cup medals– one short of the record established nearly a century ago .
- Has played 113 times for his club, Shannon, in the All Ireland League;
- His 28 AIB tries (seven in total against Lansdowne) over twelve seasons ranks him in 14 th place in the overall top try scorers list.
- Is the leading forward try-scorer in the all-time AIB statistics.

	Shannon; finishes season as the top try-scoring (16 tries) forward in the league after seven seasons.
1997/98	Munster Senior Cup medal (7); Shannon win fourth successive AIB title; plays in all 15 encounters and scores another six tries, including a hat-trick against O. Crescent.
1998/99	Plays in all eleven Shannon AIB games, scores two tries.
1999/2K	Munster Senior Cup medal (8); plays in eight of Shannon's eleven AIB outings, missing three games due to Munster's Heineken Cup successes.
2K/2001	Munster Senior Cup medal (9); marks his 100th AIB appearance with a try (his 25th AIB League try) against Terenure College on December 16th at Thomond Park.
2001 / 02	Shannon win their fifth AIB League title. Galwey plays in three of the 17 games including the semi-final and final play-offs; misses the Munster Senior Cup final due to preparations for the Heineken Cup final the following Saturday.

SUMMARY

- Has won five AIB League medals with Shannon in twelve seasons.
- Has won nine Munster Senior Cup medals– one short of the record established nearly a century ago .
- Has played 113 times for his club, Shannon, in the All Ireland League;
- His 28 AIB tries (seven in total against Lansdowne) over twelve seasons ranks him in 14 th place in the overall top try scorers list.
- Is the leading forward try-scorer in the all-time AIB statistics.

APPENDIX FOUR

HONOURS AT CLUB LEVEL

ALL STATISTICS UP TO 01 / 08 / 2002

1985/86 Munster Senior League medal (1); Munster Senior Cup medal (1).

1986/87 Munster Senior Cup medal (2).

1987/88 Munster Senior Cup medal (3).

1988/89 Munster Senior League medal (2).

1990/91 Munster Senior Cup medal (4); plays in seven of Shannon's eight AIB games – misses last game, 26/1, in Ballymena as he is rested prior to his first Ireland cap the following Saturday.

1991/92 Munster Senior Cup medal (5); plays in all eight Shannon AIB games; scores three tries; finishes up as joint top try scorer after the first two seasons.

1992/93 Captain of Shannon RFC; plays in all eight Shannon AIB games.

1993/94 - Plays in all ten Shannon games.

1994/95 With a 100% record, Shannon win AIB League for the first time ; plays in all ten games, scores two tries.

1995/96 Munster Senior Cup medal (6); Shannon retain AIB League; plays in all ten games.

1996/97 Third year in succession, Shannon win AIB League; scores six tries and plays in eleven of the 13 matches (a back injury causes him to miss the O. Wesley and O. Belvedere outings); had played in 52 consecutive AIB games for

BRIDGEND (W16-12) (A),
BRIDGEND (W40-6) (MP),
HARLEQUINS (W51-17) t (TP), CASTRES (W13-21) (A),
STADE FRANCAIS (QF, W16-14) (A),
CASTRES (SF, W25-17) (BEZIERS),
LEICESTER (F, L 9-15) (CARDIFF). 9

45

LEGEND:

t	scored try	QF	quarter-final
SF	semi-final	TP	Thomond Park
F	final	MP	Musgrave Park
		A	away game

SUMMARY:

- Has captained Munster in two Heineken Cup Finals, three semi-finals (all in France) and four quarter-finals. (two in France, two in Limerick)
- Has captained Munster in 43 of the 45 Heineken / European Cup games. Pat Murray (Shannon) was captain in 1995/96.
- Has scored nine tries in European competition which ranks him as the second leading Irish provincial try scorer in the European / Heineken Cup, 1995 – 2002.
- The 31-9 victory over Bath at Thomond Park on Saturday October 21 2000 marked Mick Galwey's 100th appearance in a Munster jersey for an officially-capped match.

PROVINCIAL STATISTICS

- The most appearances by any player for an Irish provincial side. (126 times).
- The first Irish player to win 100 official caps for his province.
- The Irish player who has captained his province the most occasions. (85 times).
- The Irish player with the most appearances in seven seasons of European competitions (45 games).

APPENDIX THREE

HONOURS AT HEINEKEN CUP LEVEL

ALL STATISTICS UP TO 01 / 08 / 2002

		Caps
1995/96	SWANSEA (W17-13) (TP), CASTRES (L12-19) (A).	2
1996/97	MILAN (W23-5) (MP), CARDIFF (L18-48)(A), WASPS (W49-22) t (TP), TOULOUSE (L19-60) (A).	4
1997/98	HARLEQUINS (L40-48) t (A), CARDIFF (L23-43) (A), BOURGOIN (W17-15) (TP), CARDIFF (L32-37) (MP), BOURGOIN (L6-21) (A), HARLEQUINS (W23-16) (TP).	6
1998/99	PADOVA (W20-13) (MP), NEATH (W34-10) 2t (MP), PERPIGNAN (L24-41) t (A), NEATH (D18-18) t (A), PERPIGNAN (W13-5) (MP), PADOVA (W35-21) (A), COLOMIERS (QF, L9-23)(A).	7
1999/2K	PONTYPRIDD (W32-10) (TP), SARACENS (W35-34) (A), COLOMIERS (W31-15) (A), COLOMIERS (W23-5)(MP), SARACENS (W31-30) t (TP), PONTYPRIDD (L36- 38) (A), STADE FRANCAIS (QF, W27-10) (TP), TOULOUSE (SF, W31-25) (BORDEAUX), NORTHAMPTON (F, L 8-9) (TWICKENHAM).	9
2K/2001	NEWPORT (W26-18) t (TP), CASTRES (W32-29) (A), BATH (W31-9) (TP)*, BATH (L5- 18) (A), NEWPORT (W39-24) (A) , CASTRES (W21-11) (MP), BIARRITZ (QF, W38- 29) (TP) STADE FRANCAIS (SF, L 15-16) (LILLE).	8
2001/ 02	CASTRES (W28-23) (TP), HARLEQUINS (W24-8) (A),	